Elizabeth Acevedo

INHERITANCE

a visual poem

art by

ANDREA PIPPINS

Quill Tree Books
An Imprint of HarperCollinsPublishers

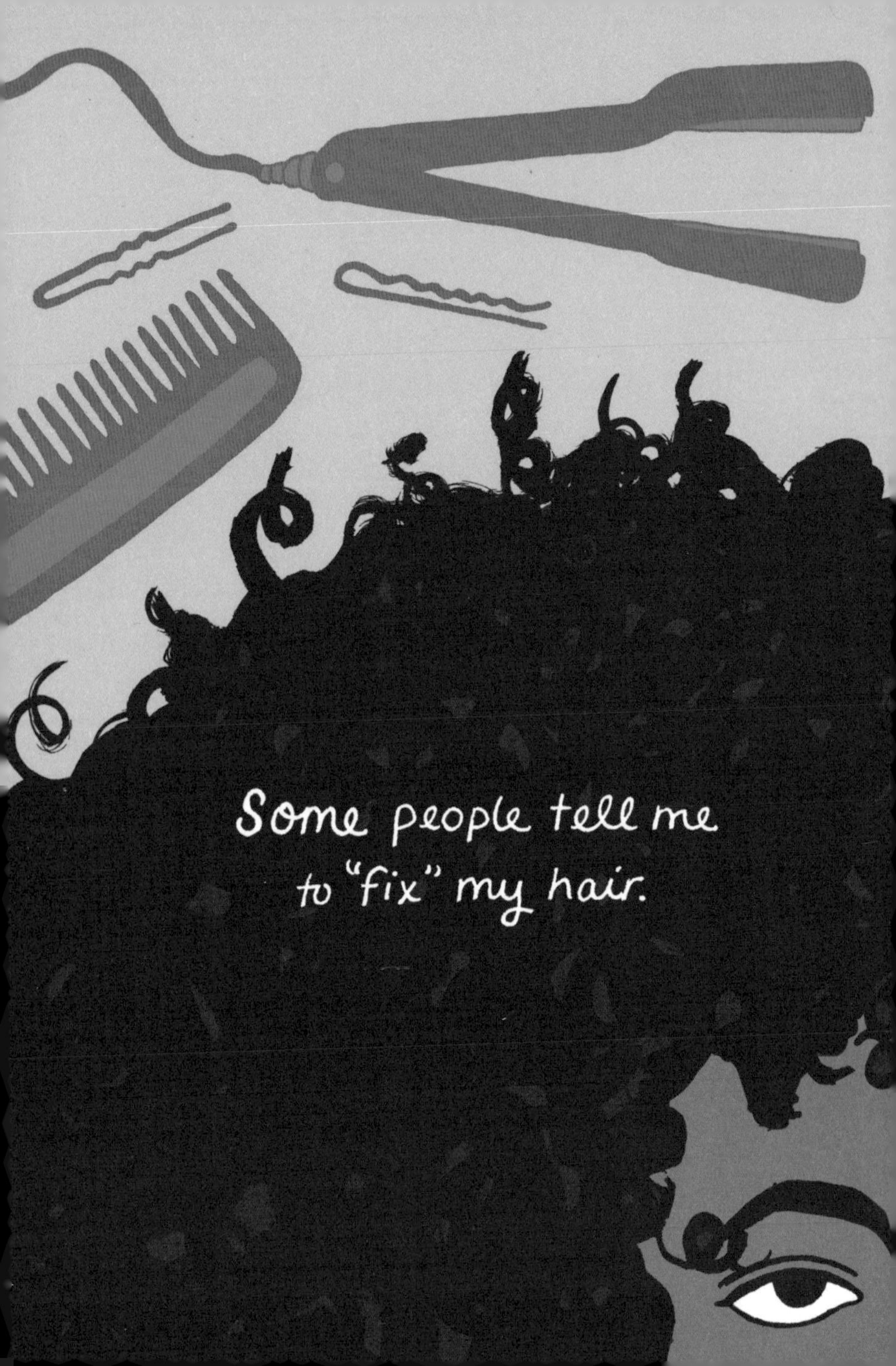
Some people tell me
to "fix" my hair.

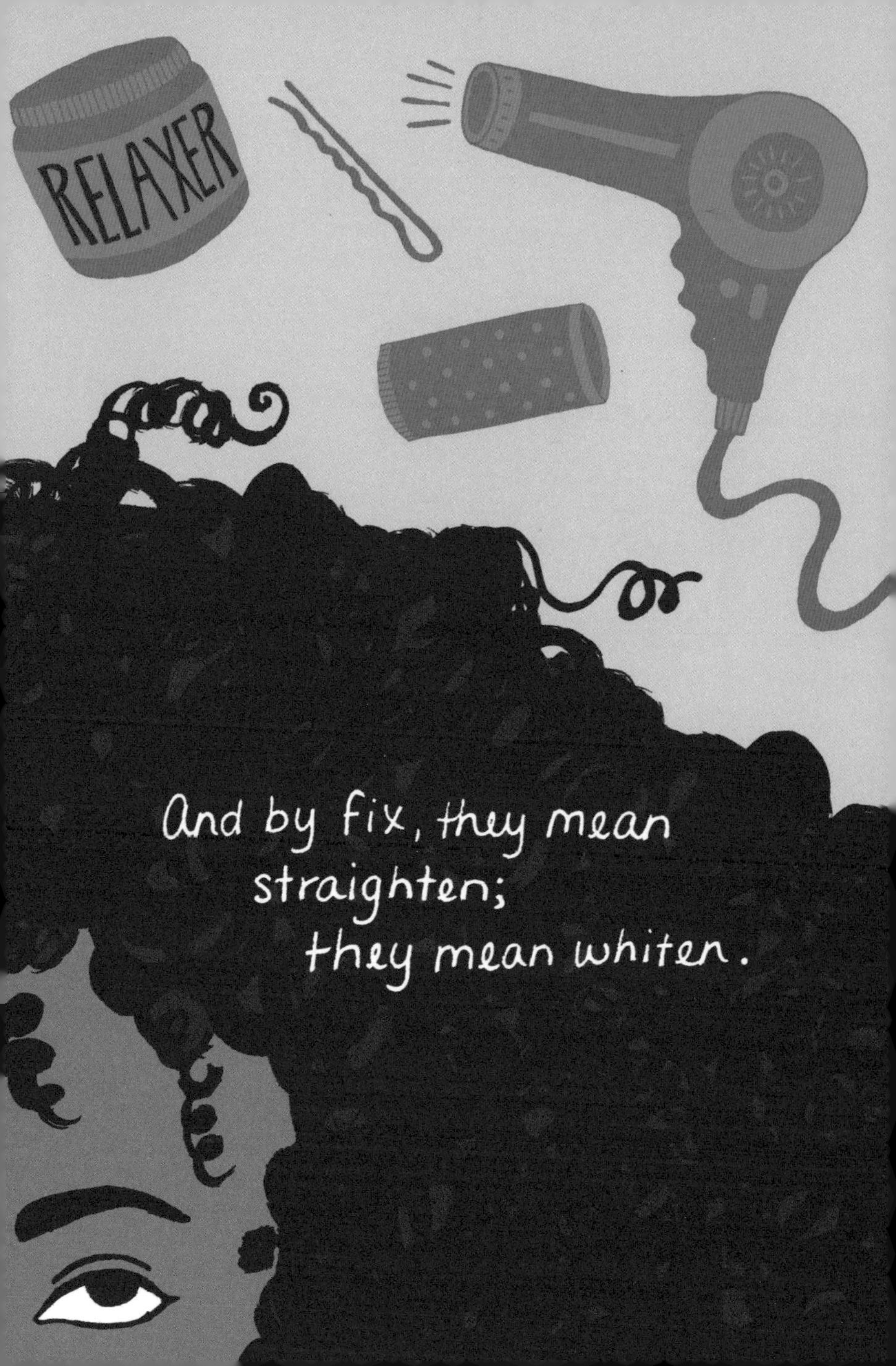
RELAXER
And by fix, they mean
straighten;
they mean whiten.

But how do you fix this shipwrecked history of hair?

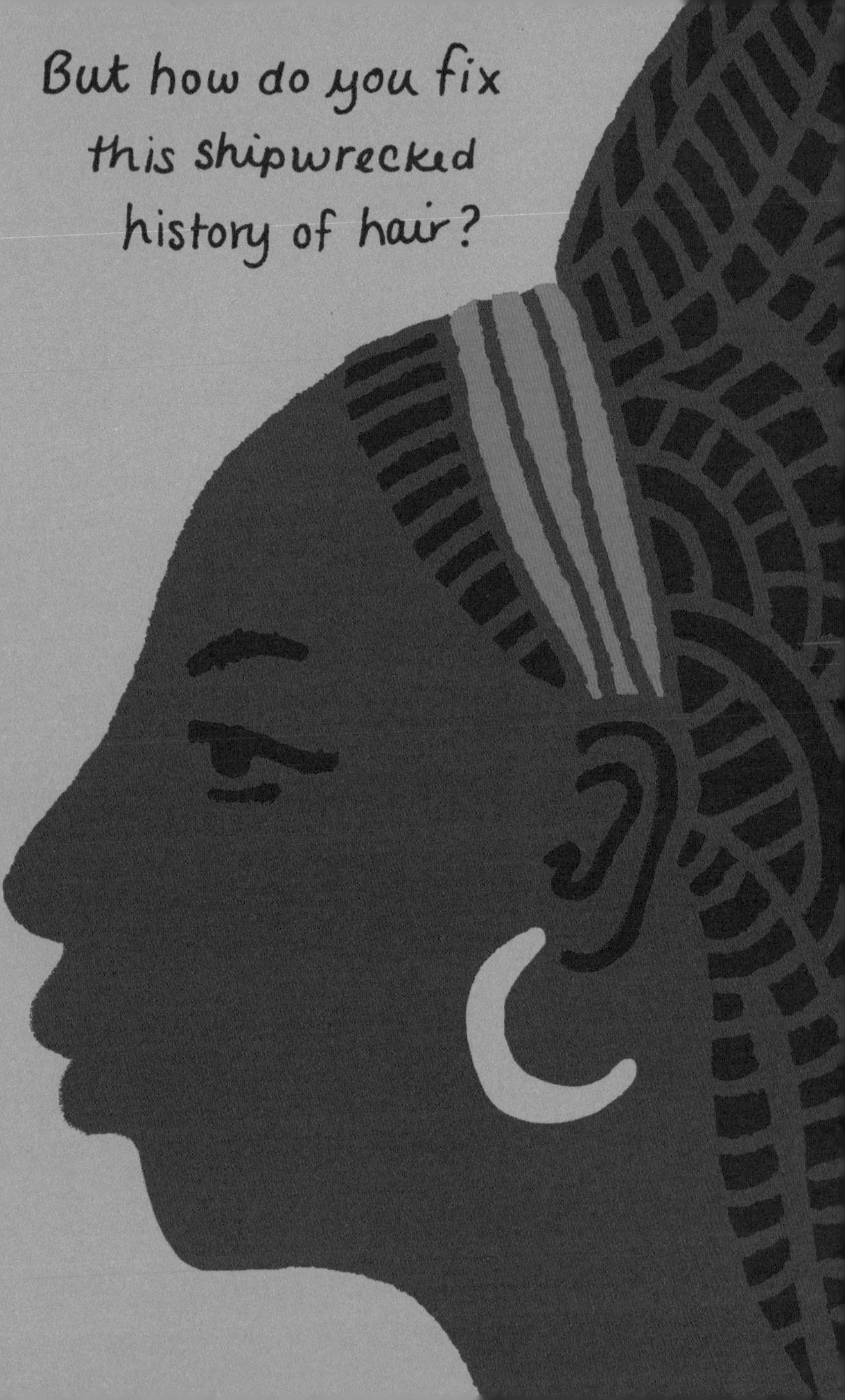

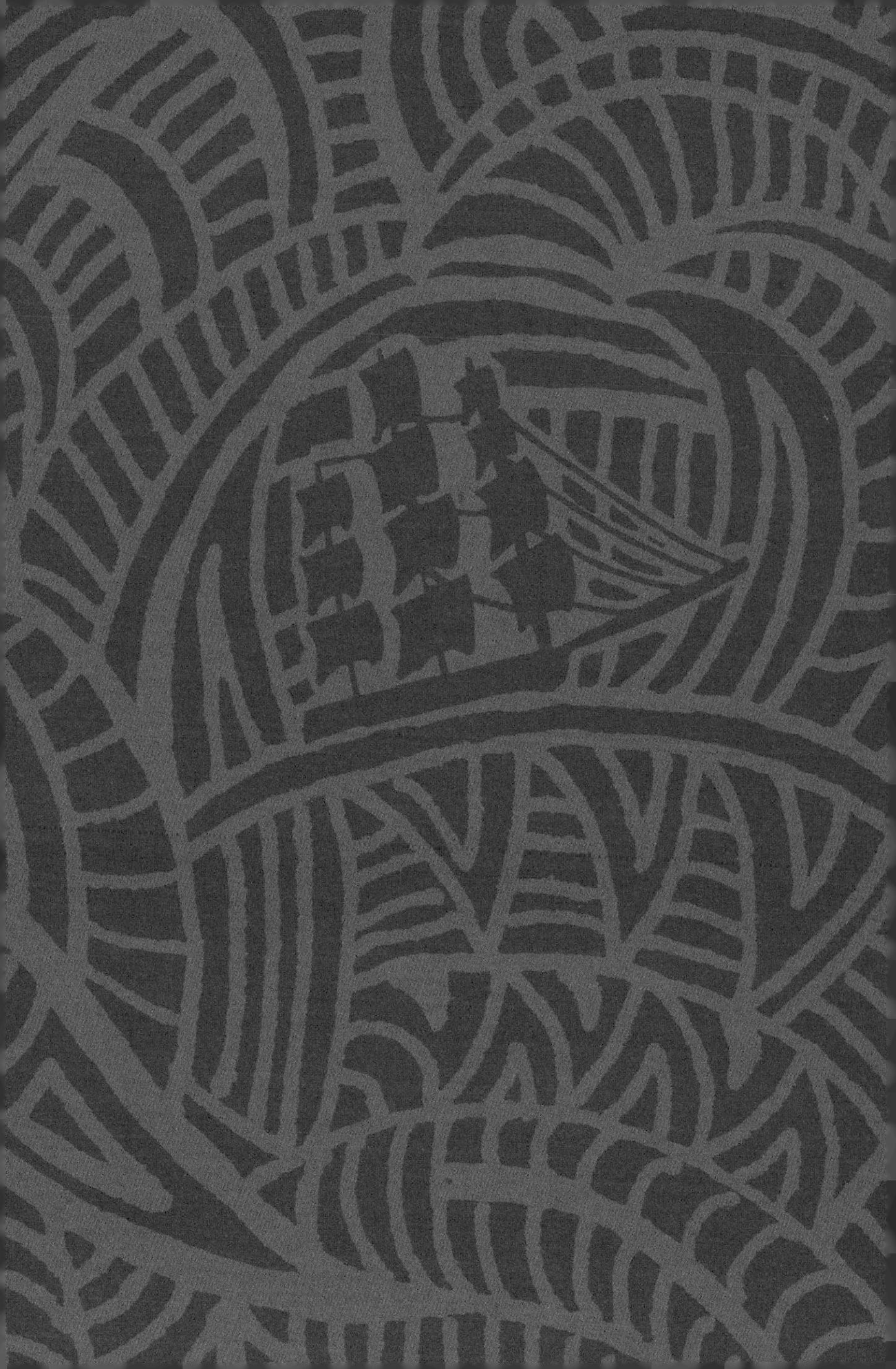

The true meaning of stranded.

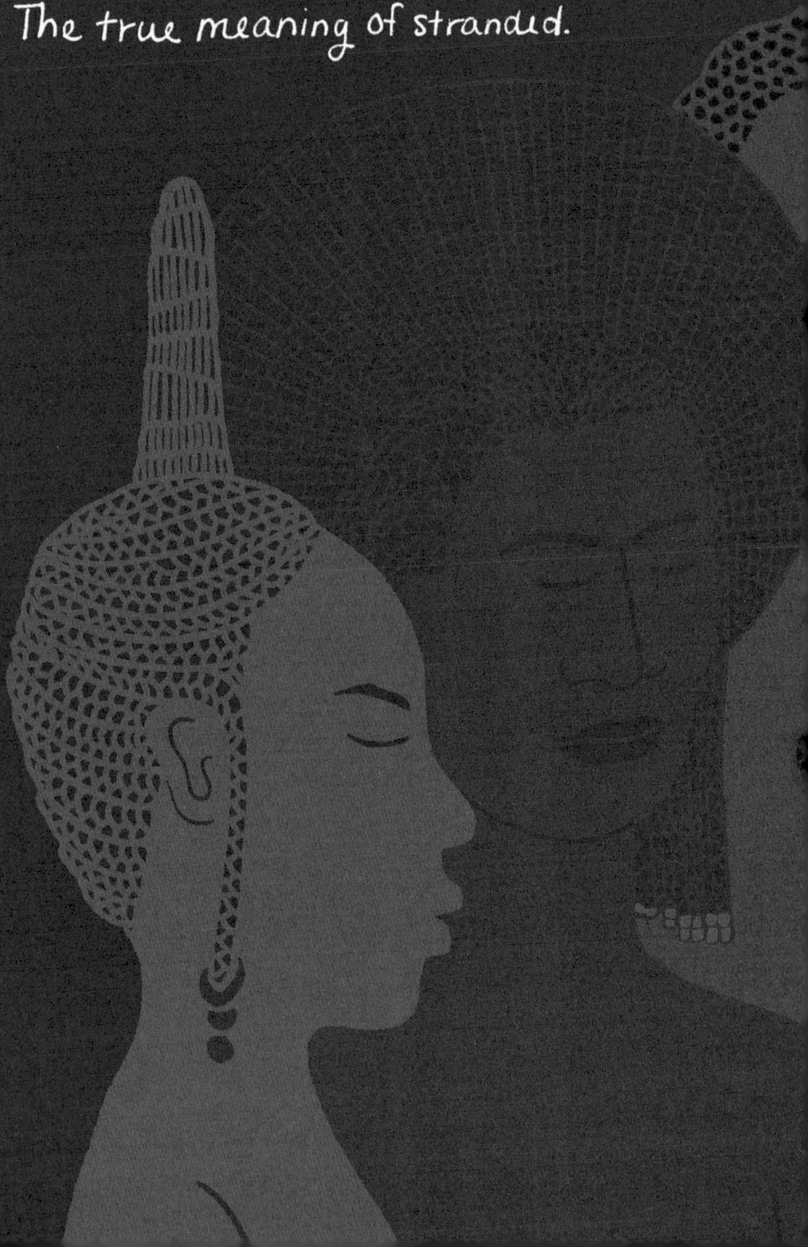

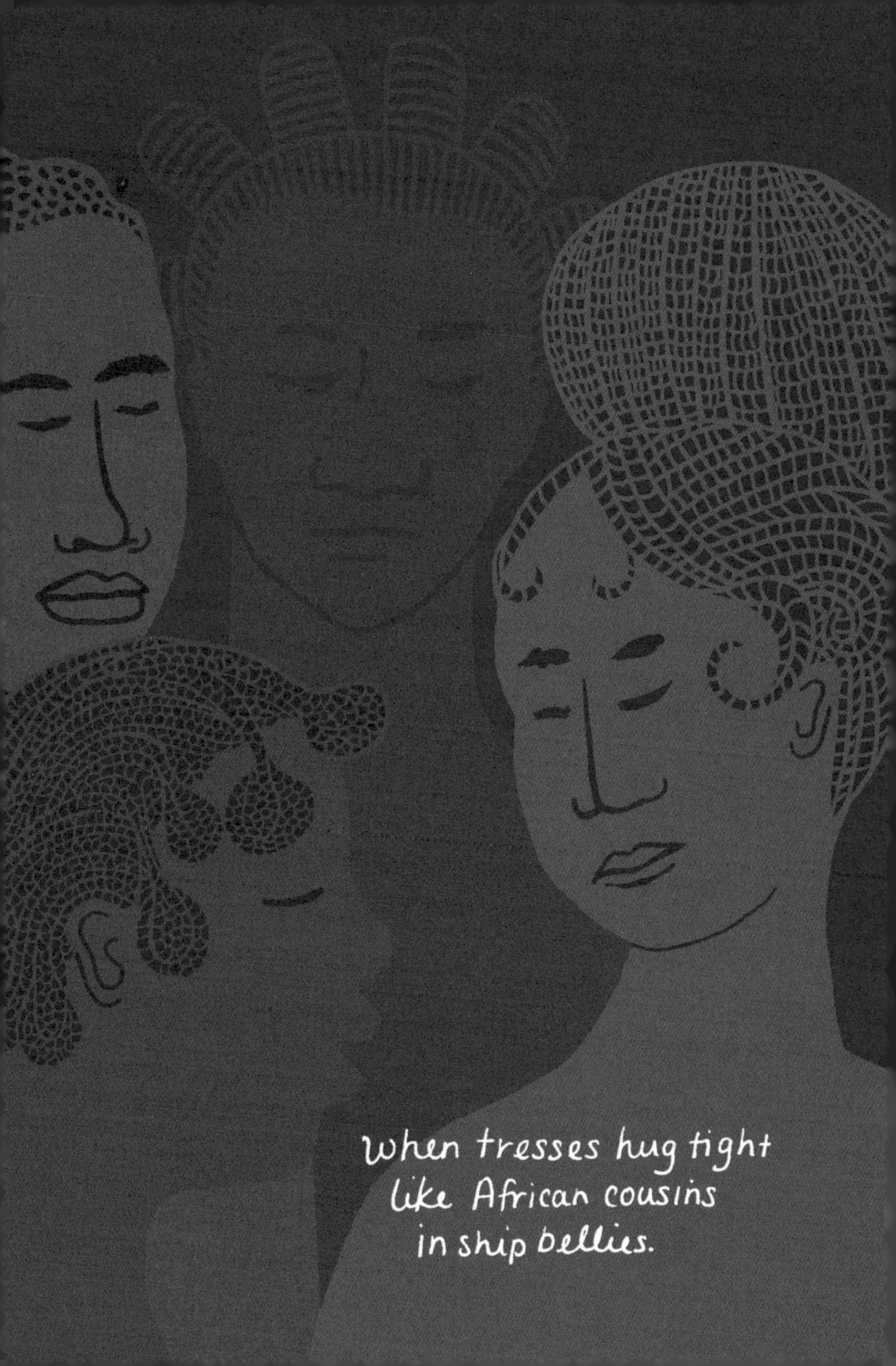
when tresses hug tight
like African cousins
in ship bellies.

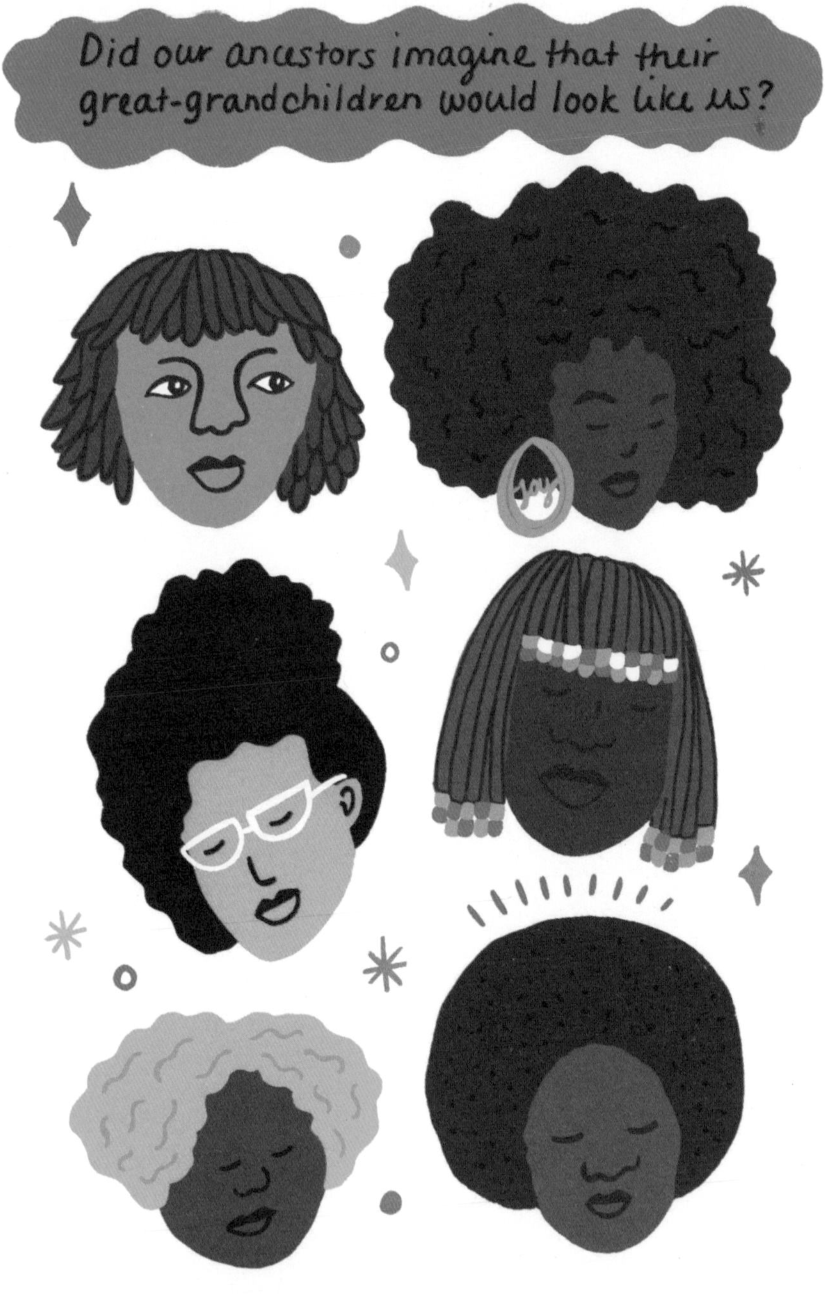
Did our ancestors imagine that their great-grandchildren would look like us?
joy

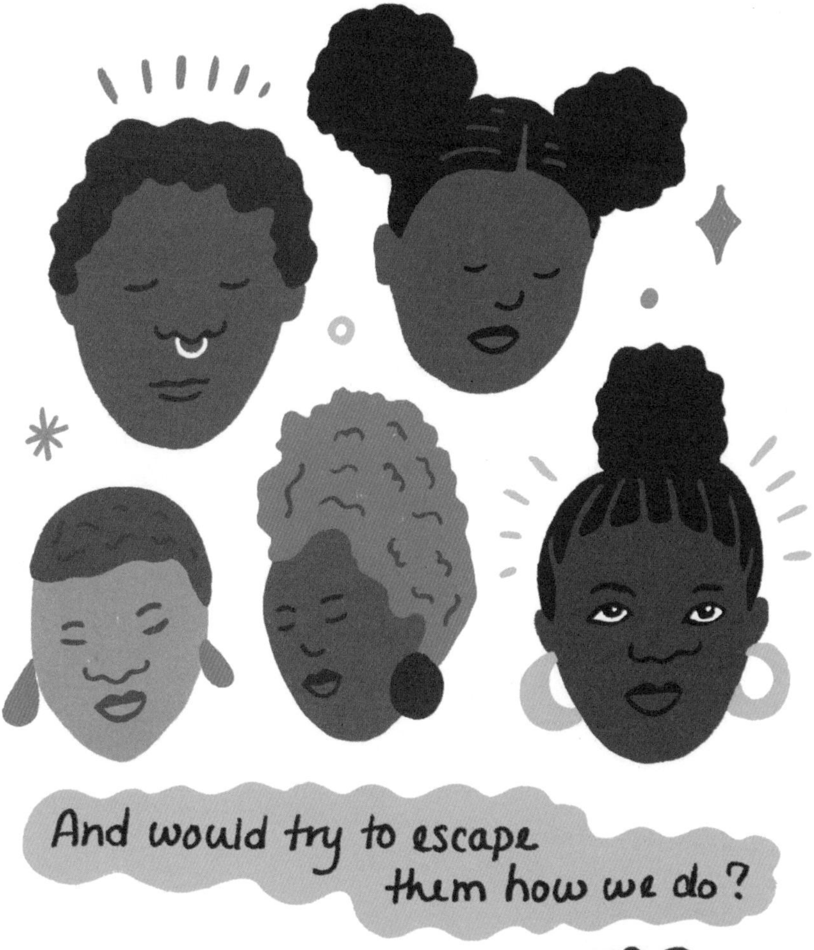

And would try to escape them how we do?

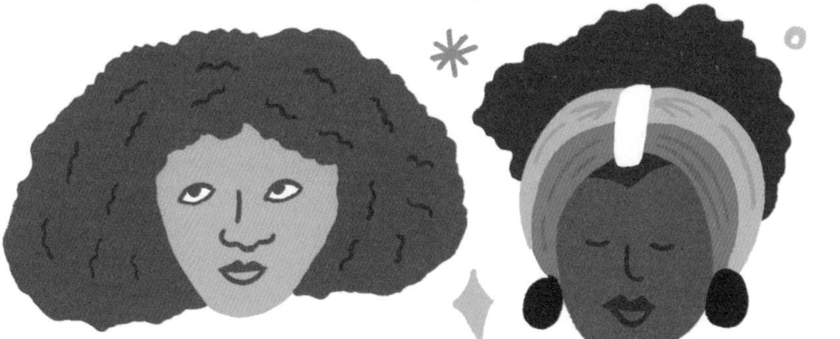

Finding ways to erase them
out from our skin,

to iron them out of our hair.

This wild
tangle of hair
that strangles air.

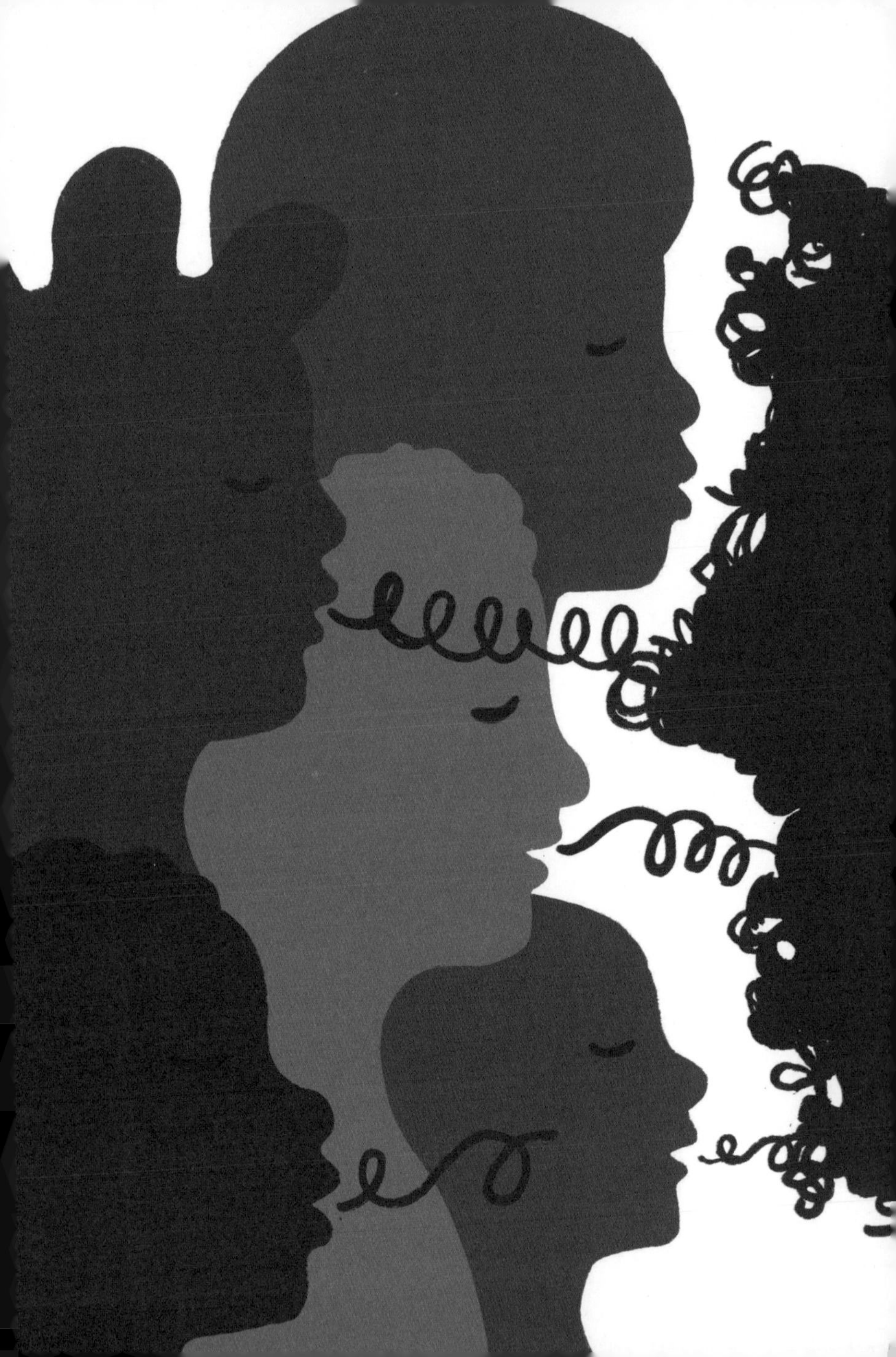

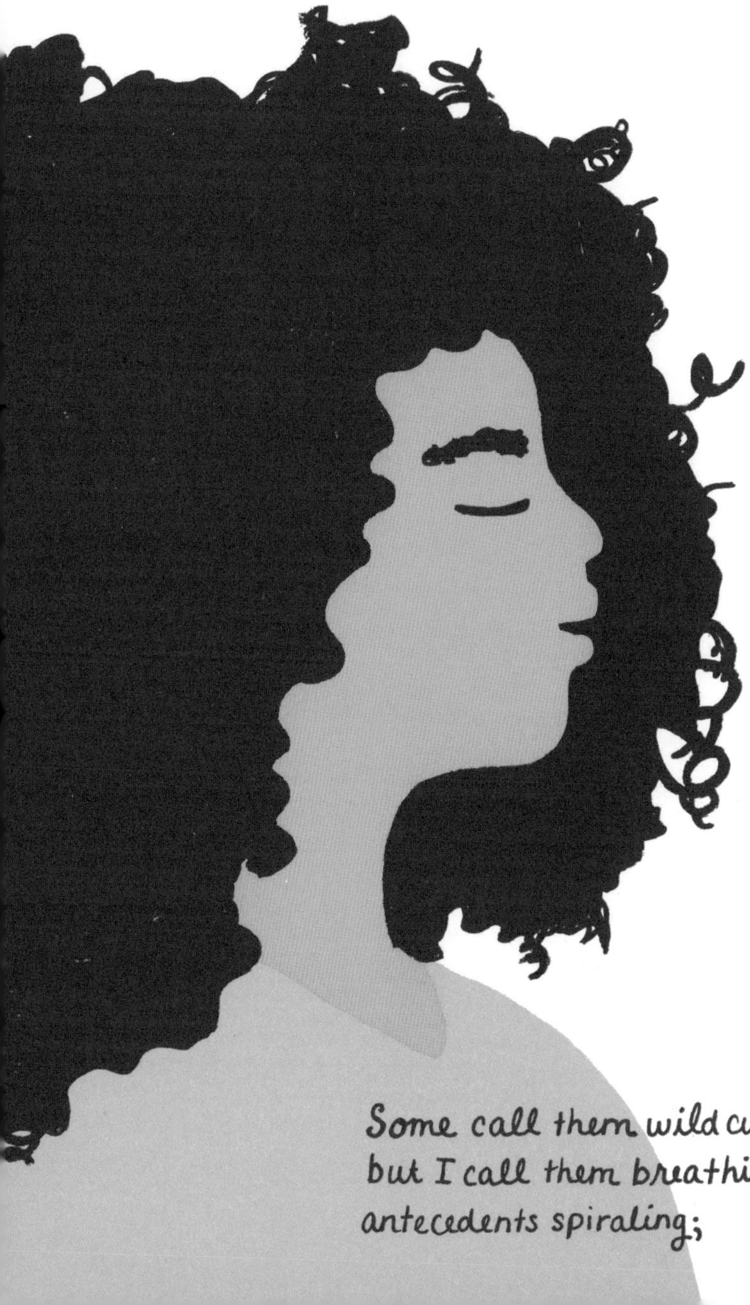

Some call them wild curls,
but I call them breathing,
antecedents spiraling;

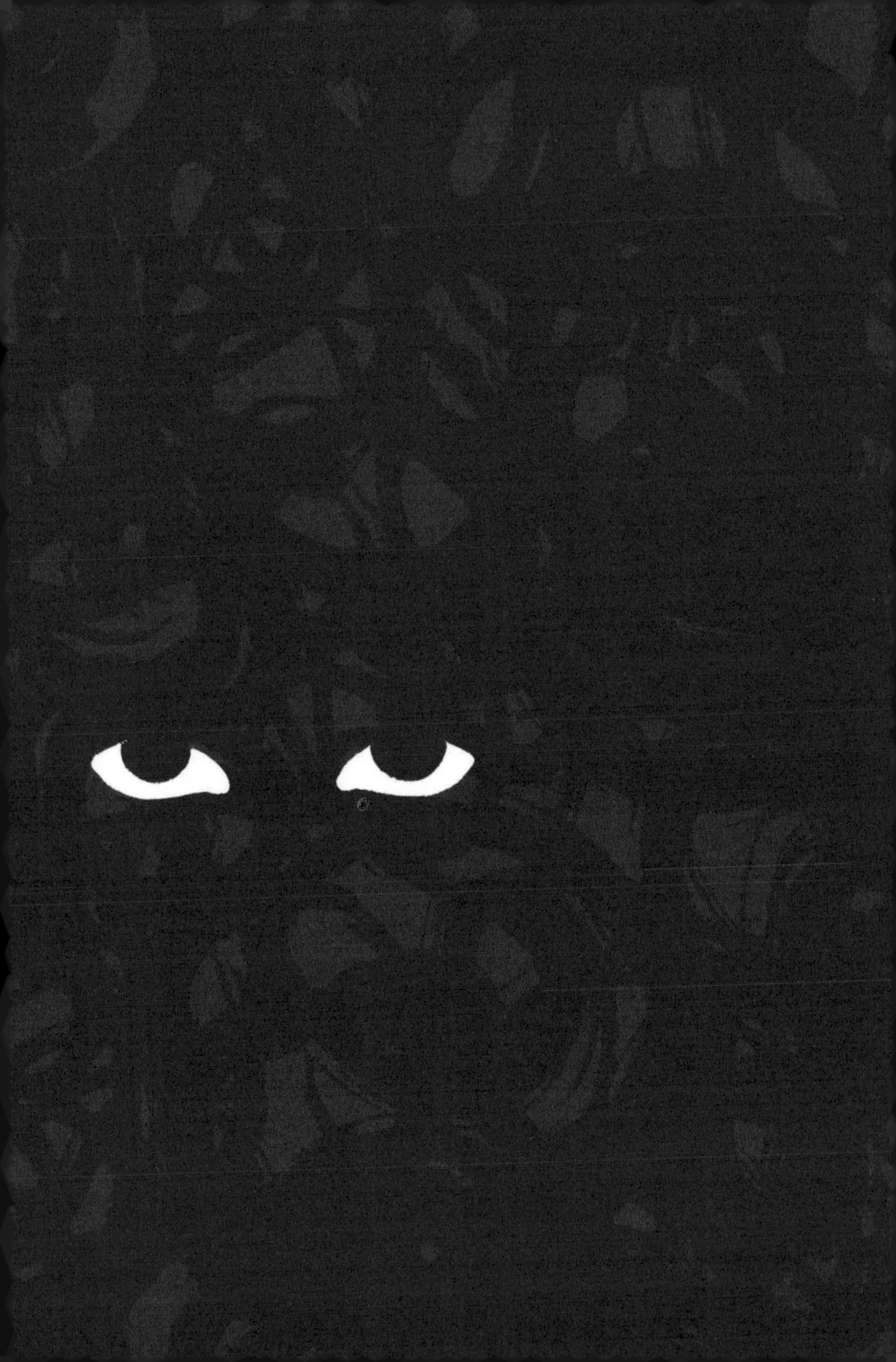

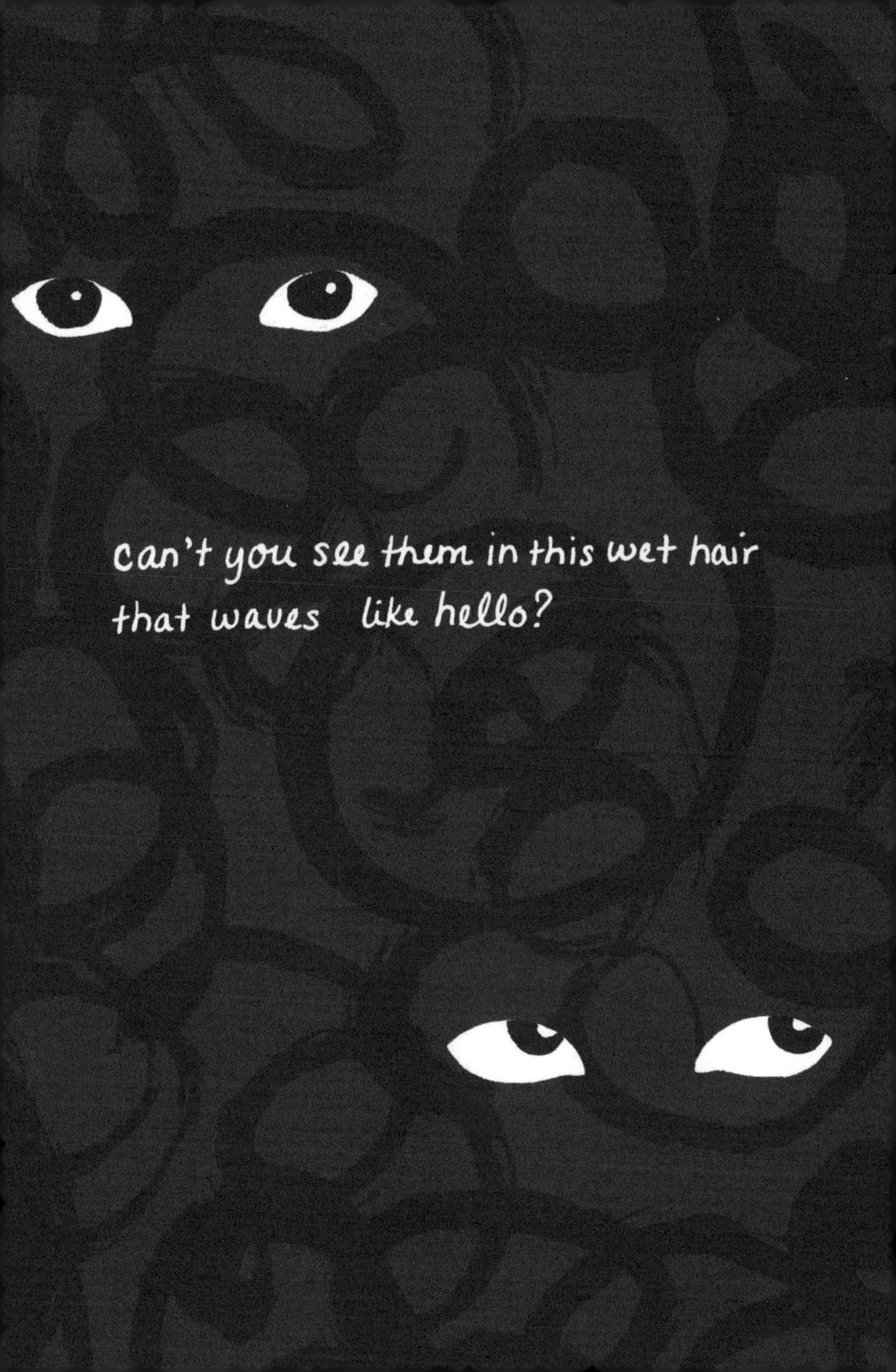
can't you see them in this wet hair
that waves like hello?

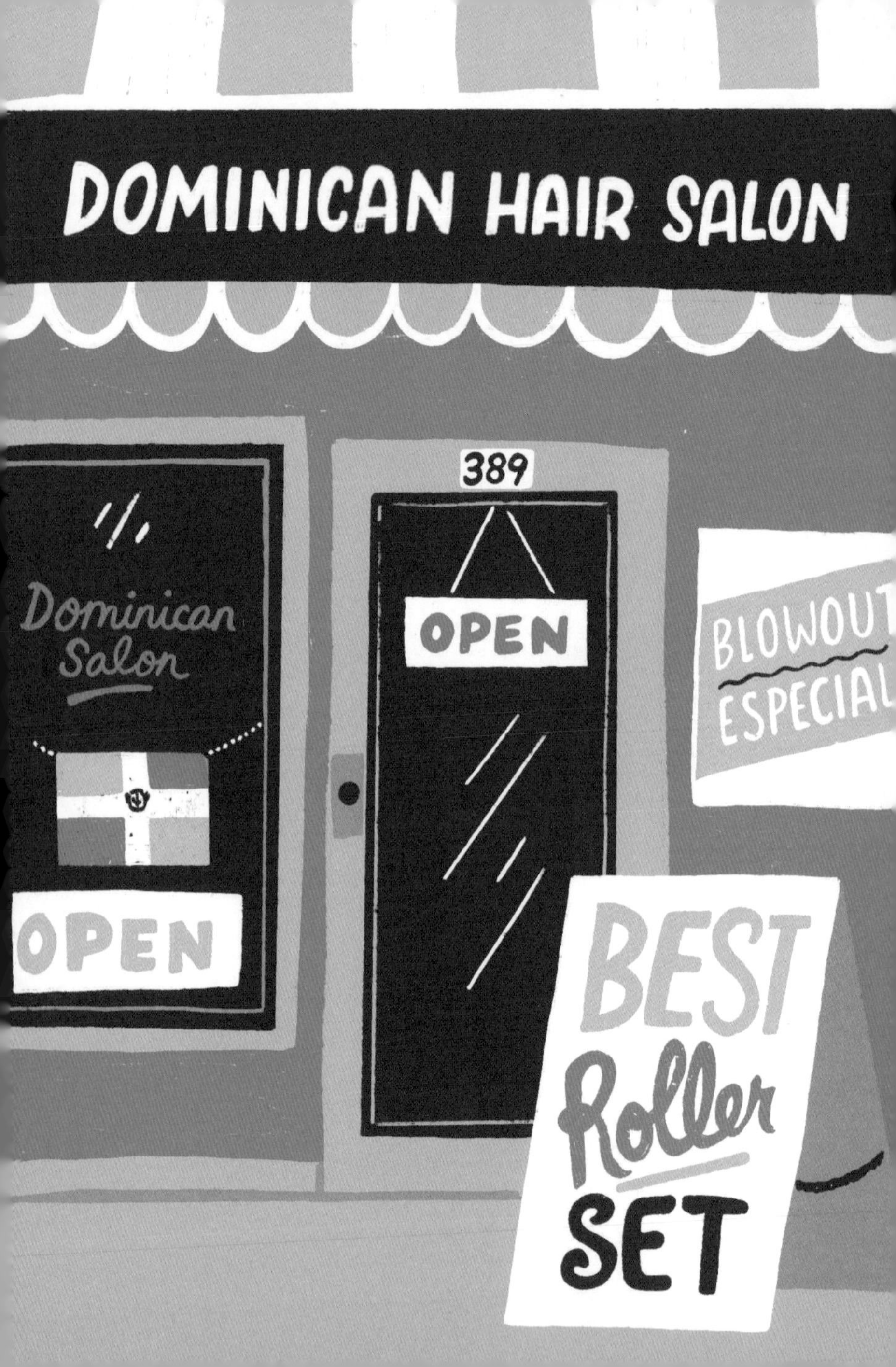
DOMINICAN HAIR SALON
Dominican Salon
OPEN
389
OPEN
BLOWOUT ESPECIAL
BEST Roller SET

We're told Dominicans do the best hair.
We can wash, set, flatten the spring in any lock.

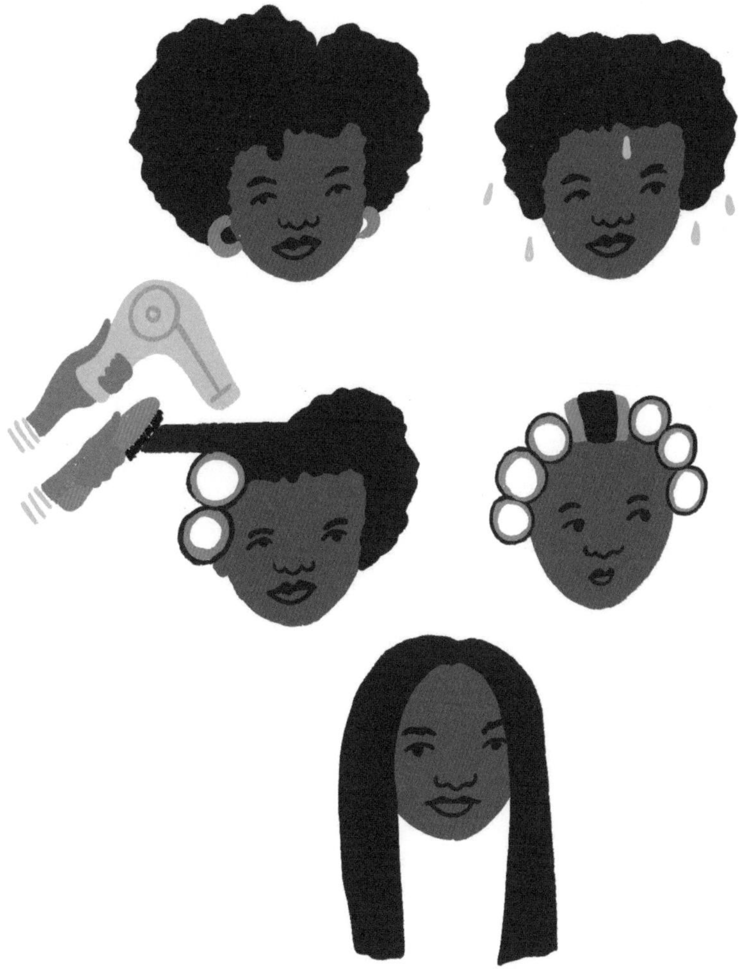

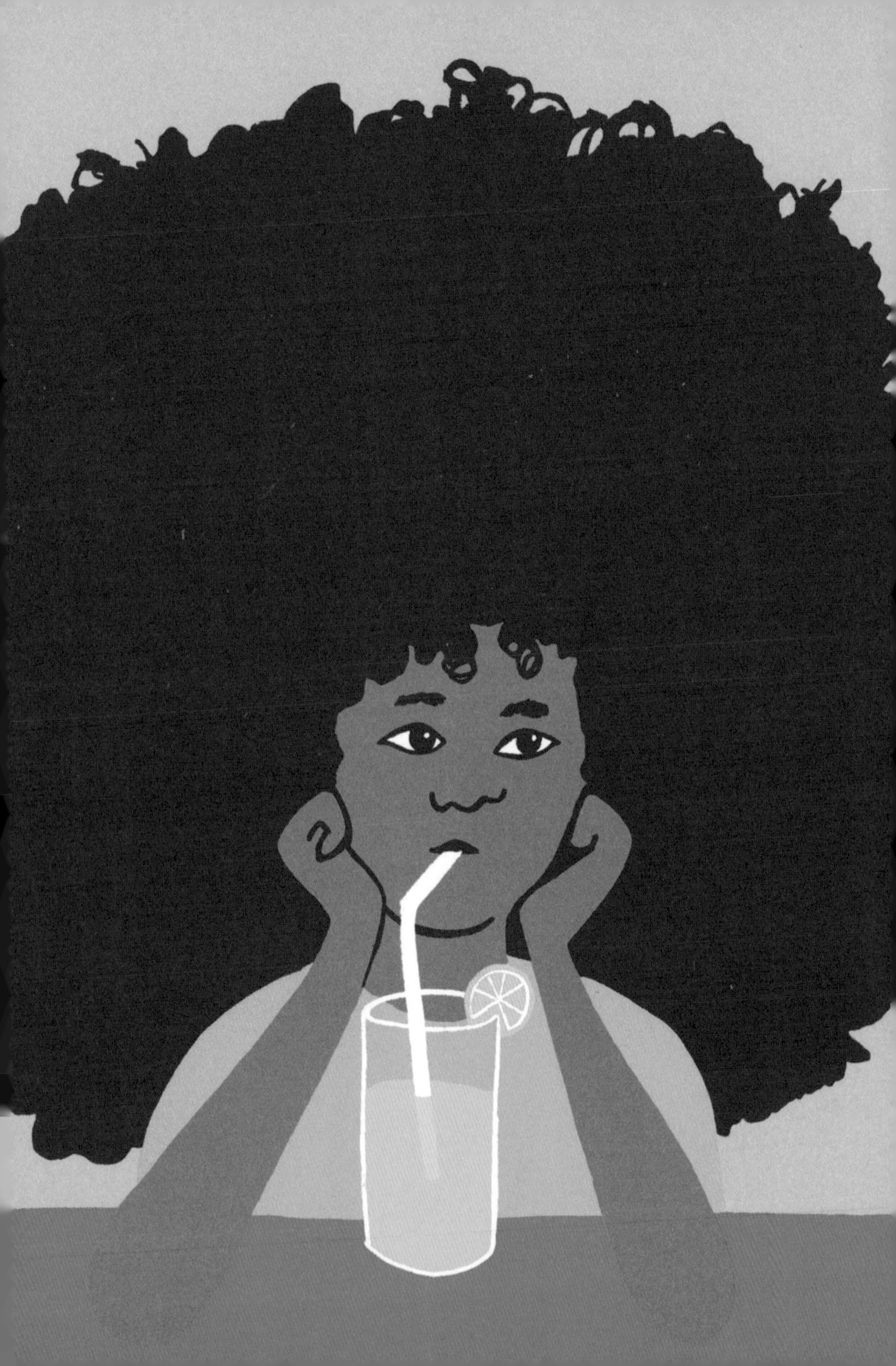

BUT WHAT THEY MEAN IS:

We are the best at
swallowing amnesia
in a cup of morir soñando:
DIE DREAMING.

Because it seems easier
to do that than live in this
REALITY,

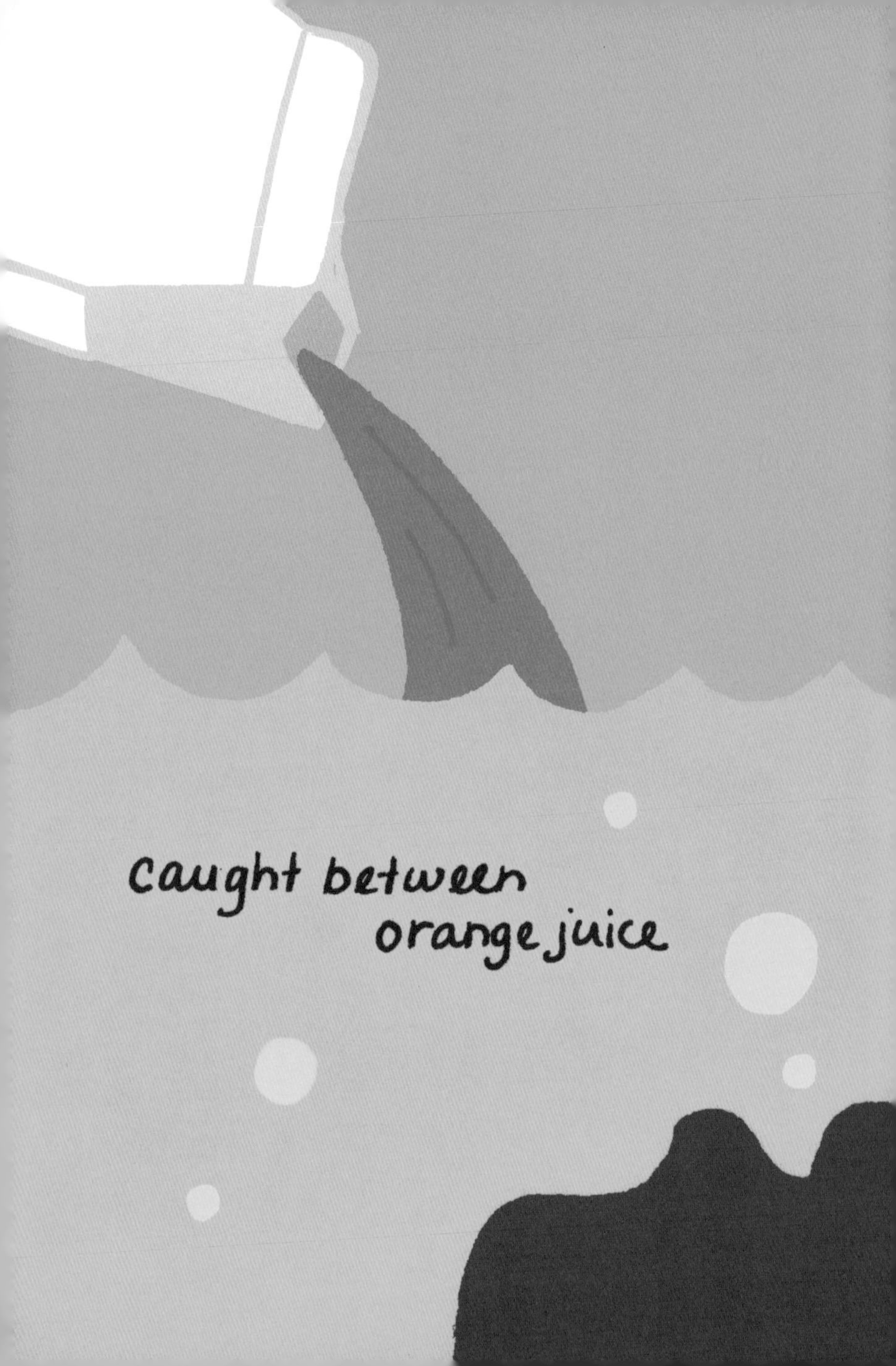
caught between
orange juice

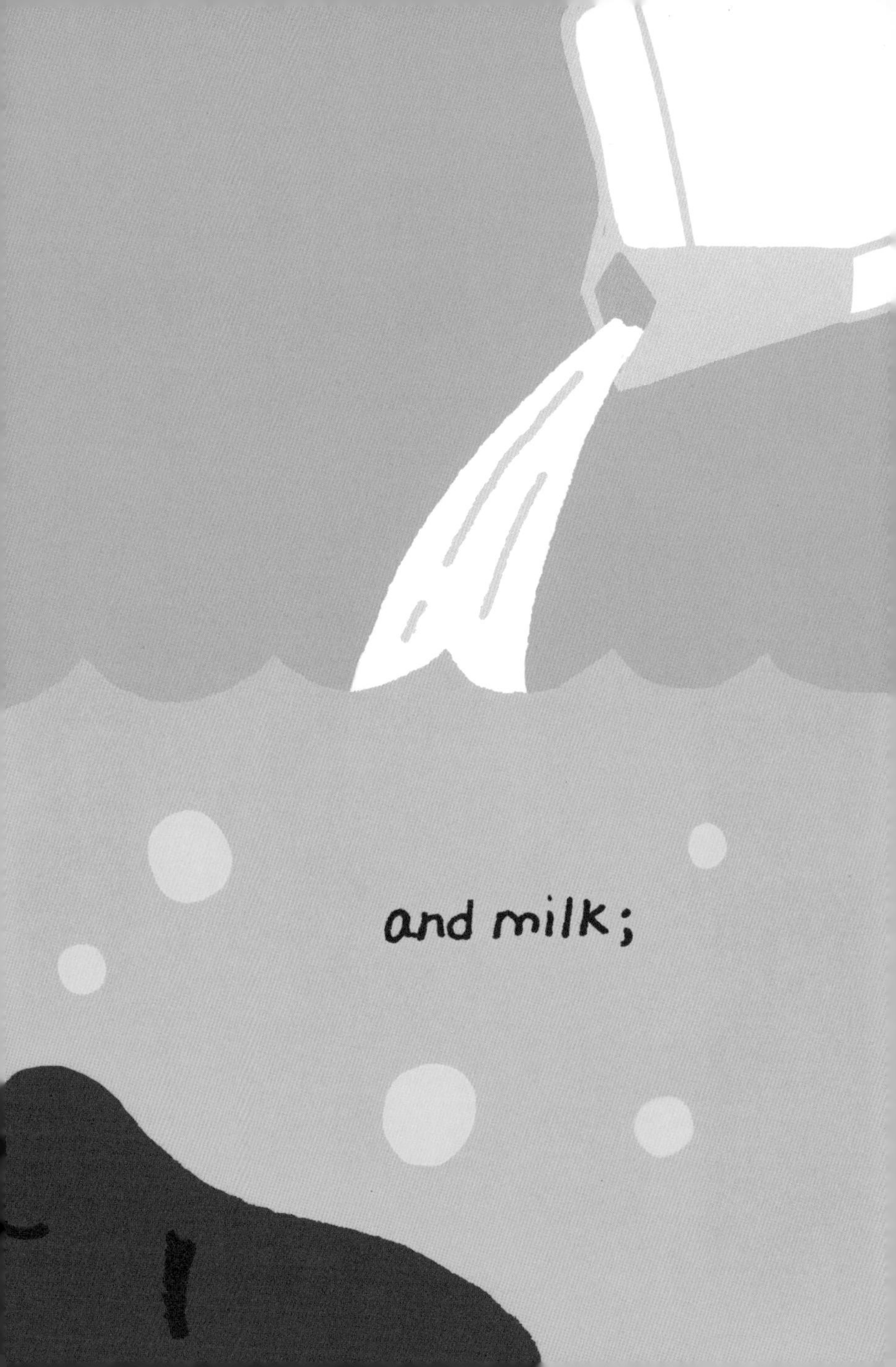
and milk;

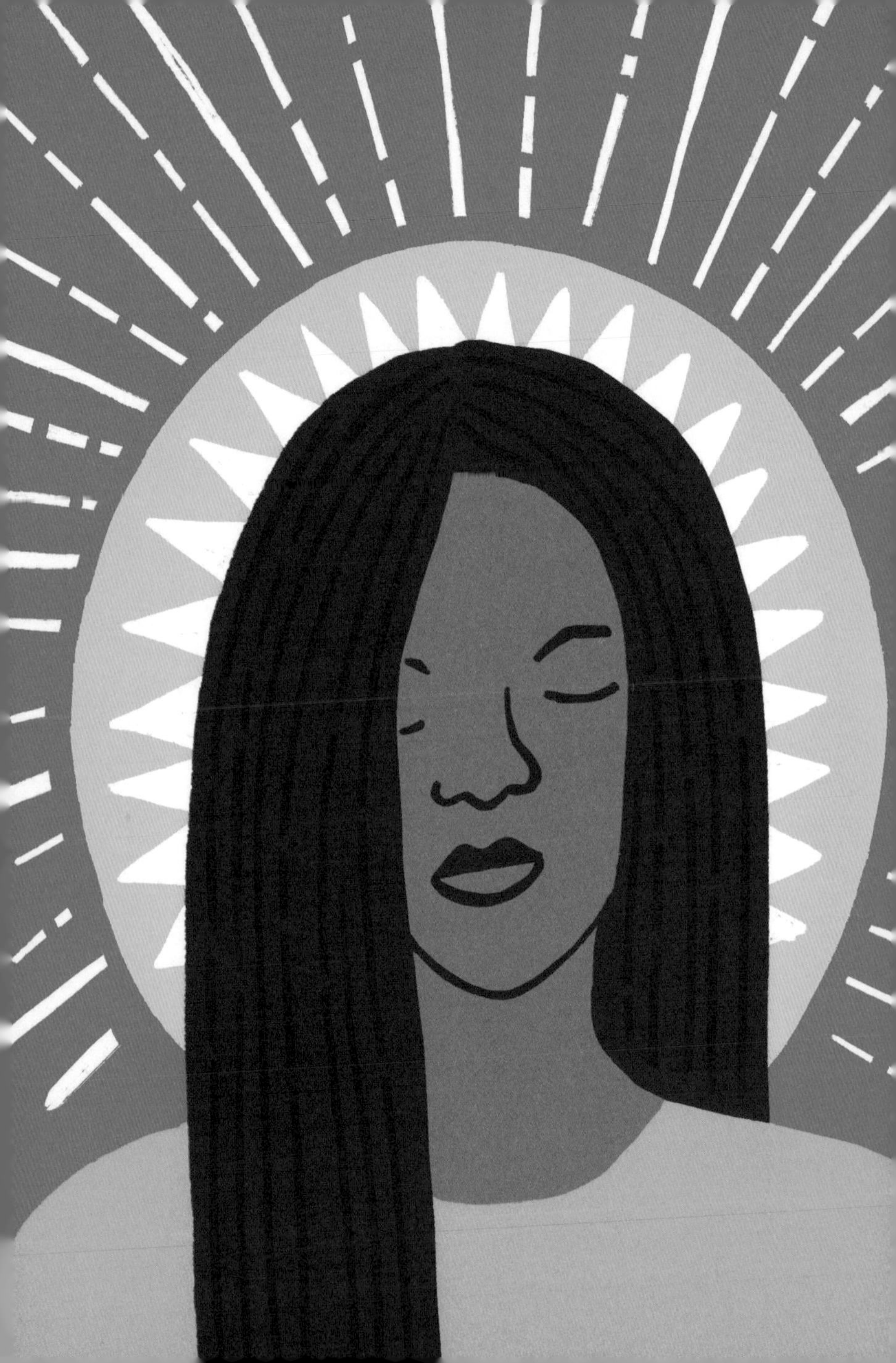

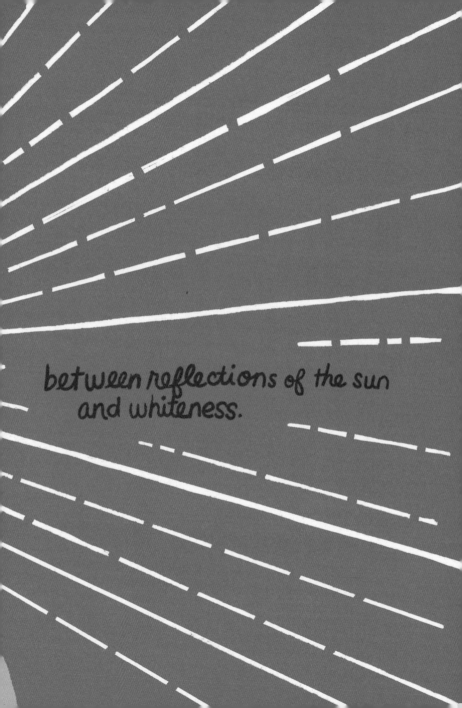

between reflections of the sun and whiteness.

What they mean is:

WHY WOULD YOU DATE A BLACK MAN?

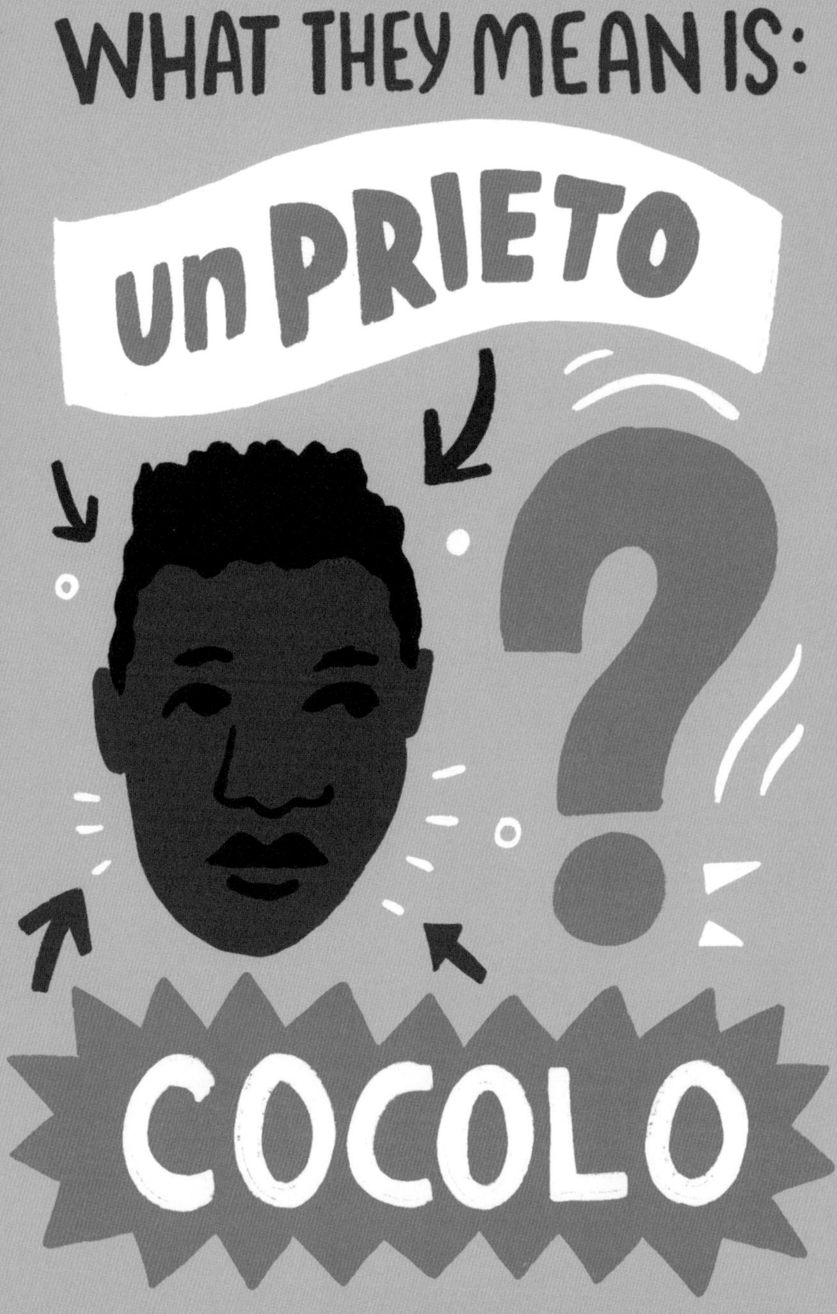
WHAT THEY MEAN IS:
un PRIETO
COCOLO

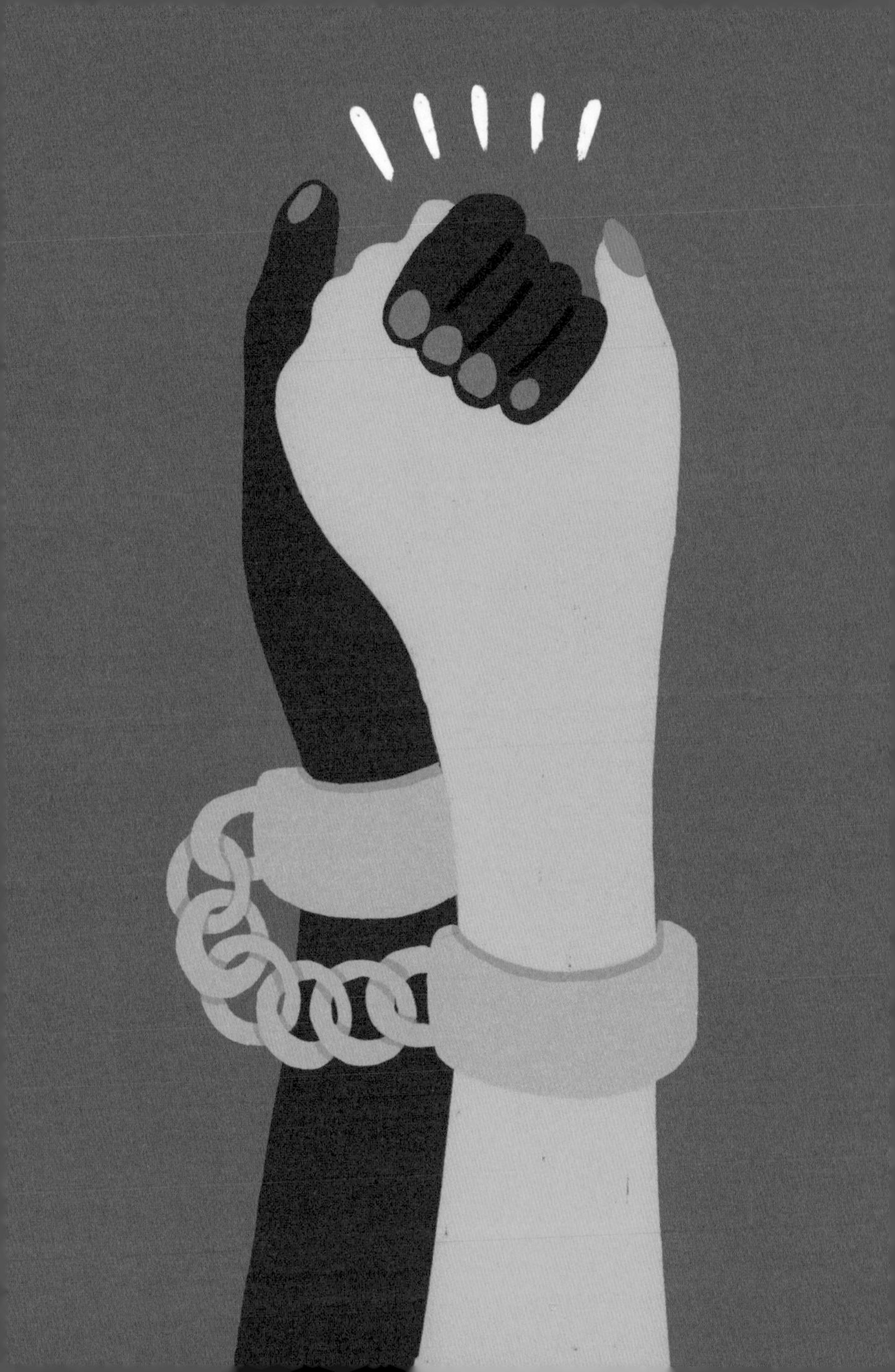

What they mean is:
Why would two
OPPRESSED
PEOPLE
come together?
It's two times
the trouble.

WHAT
REA
mean

THEY
LLY
is:

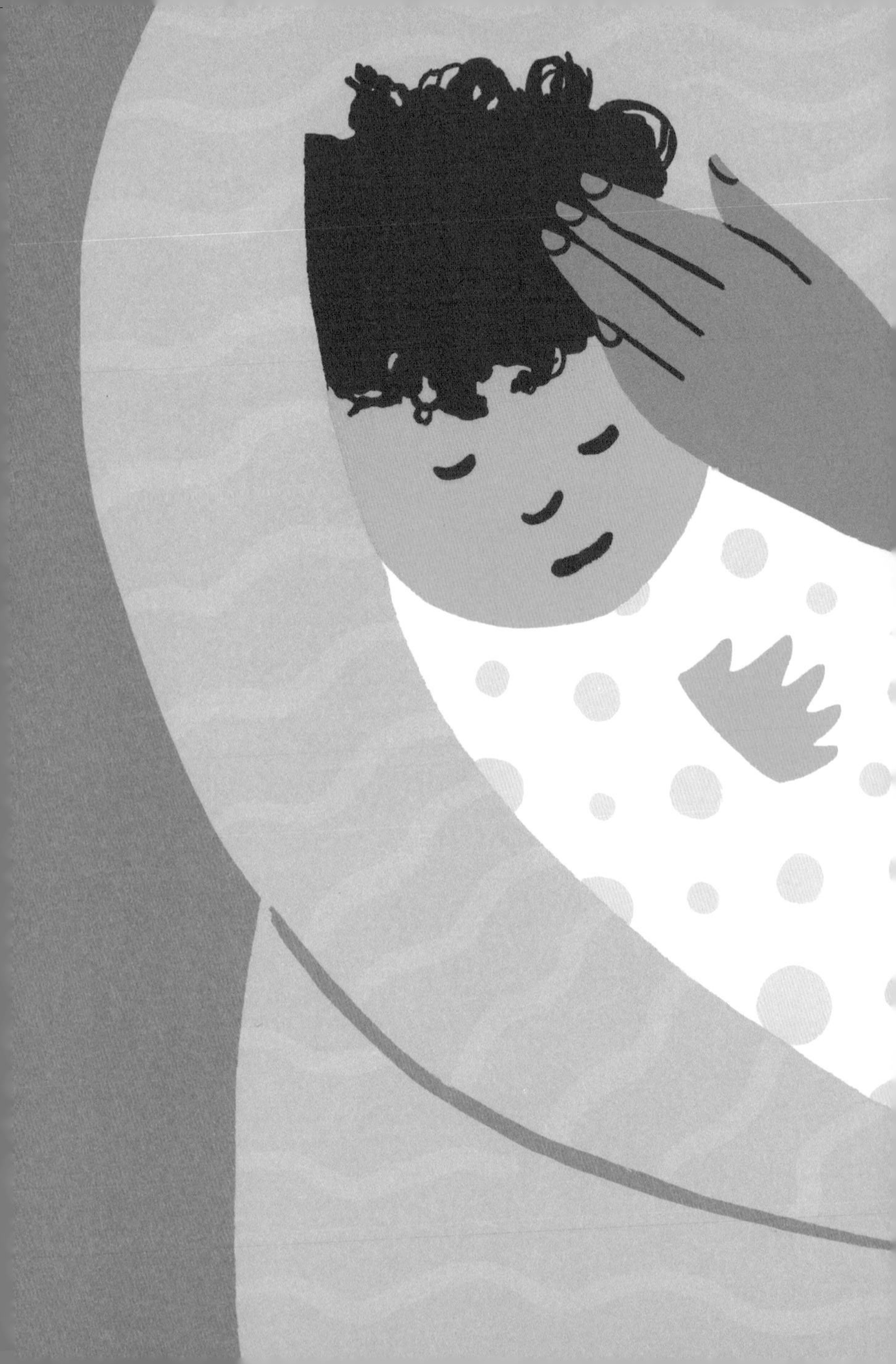

Have you thought of
your daughter's hair?

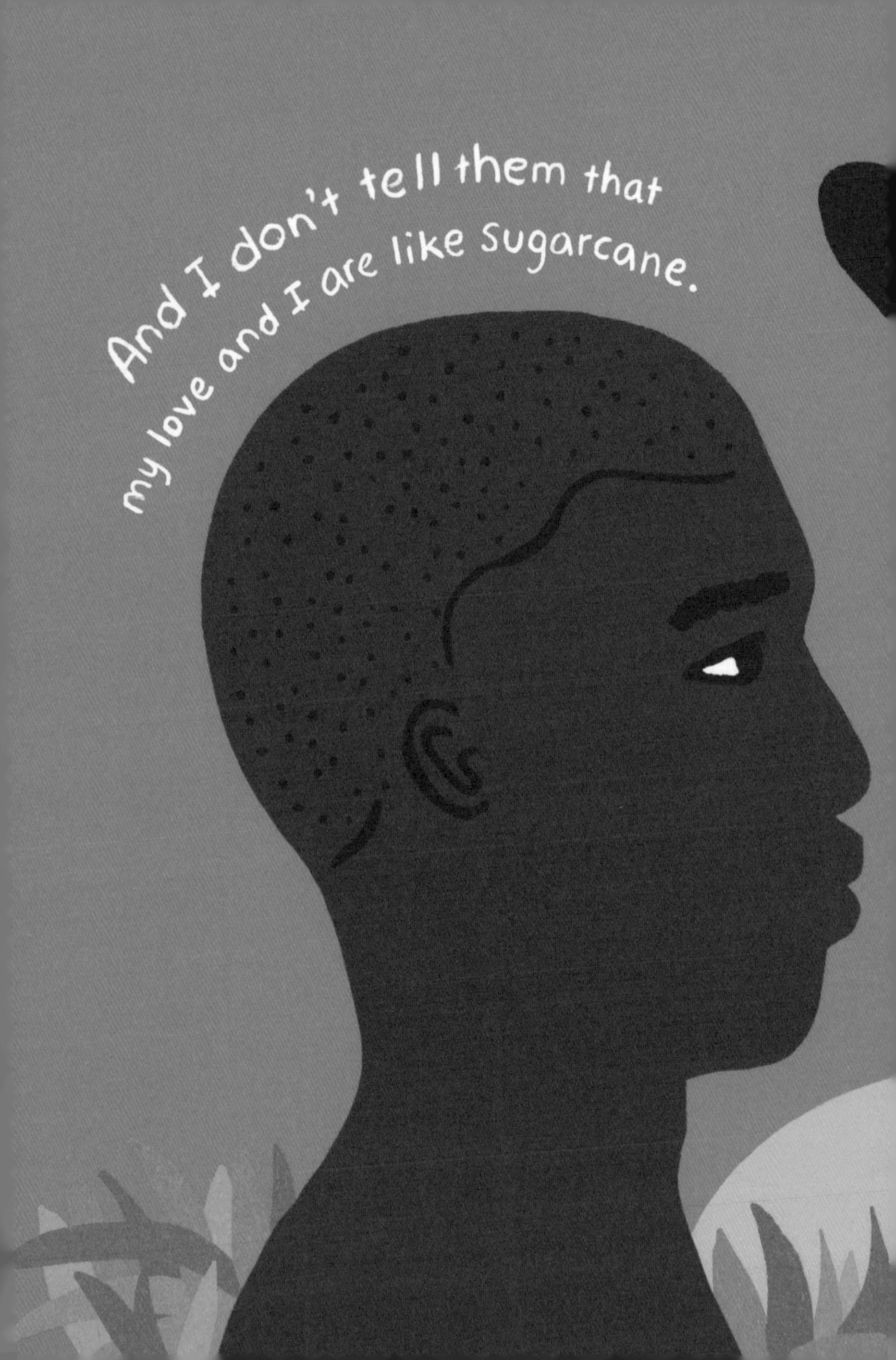

And I don't tell them that
my love and I are like sugarcane.

Dark-skinned, paler-fleshed,
meshed and pure sweetness.
The children of children of fields.

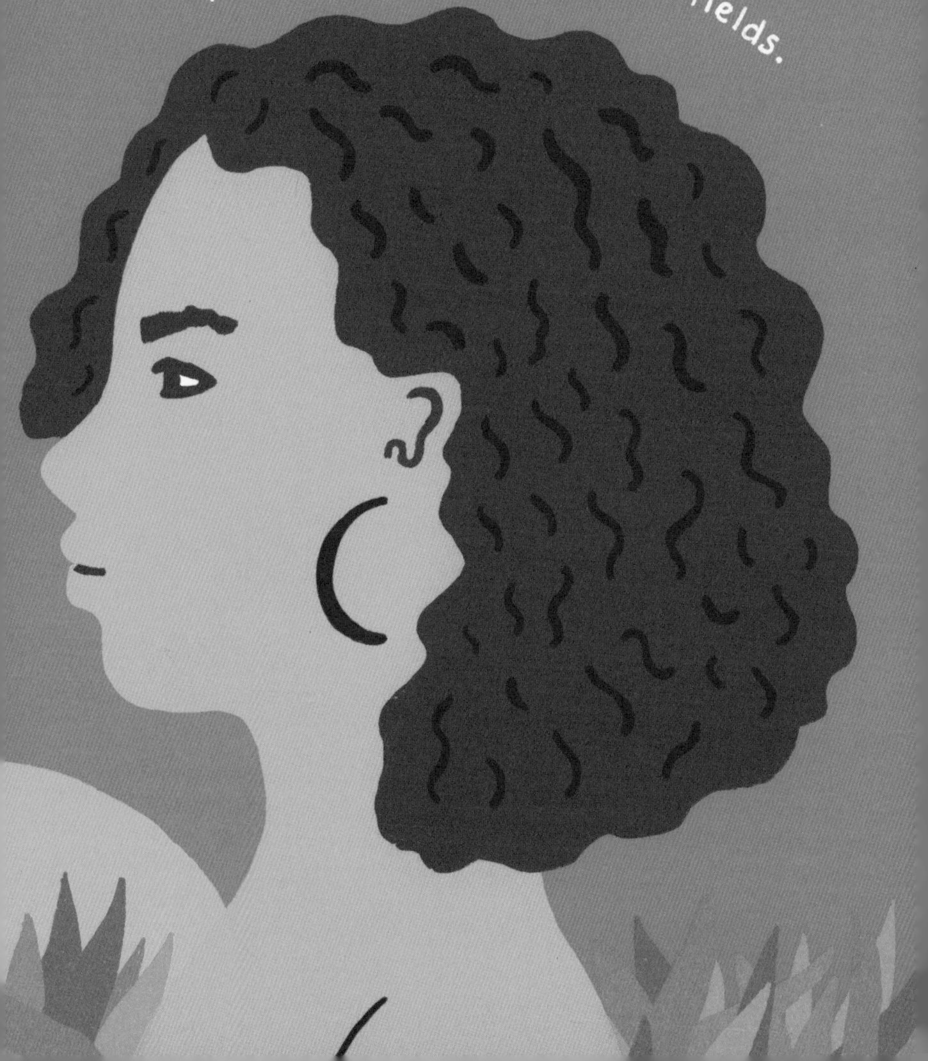

Our bodies curve
into each other like an echo,
and I let my curtain of curls
blanket us from the world.

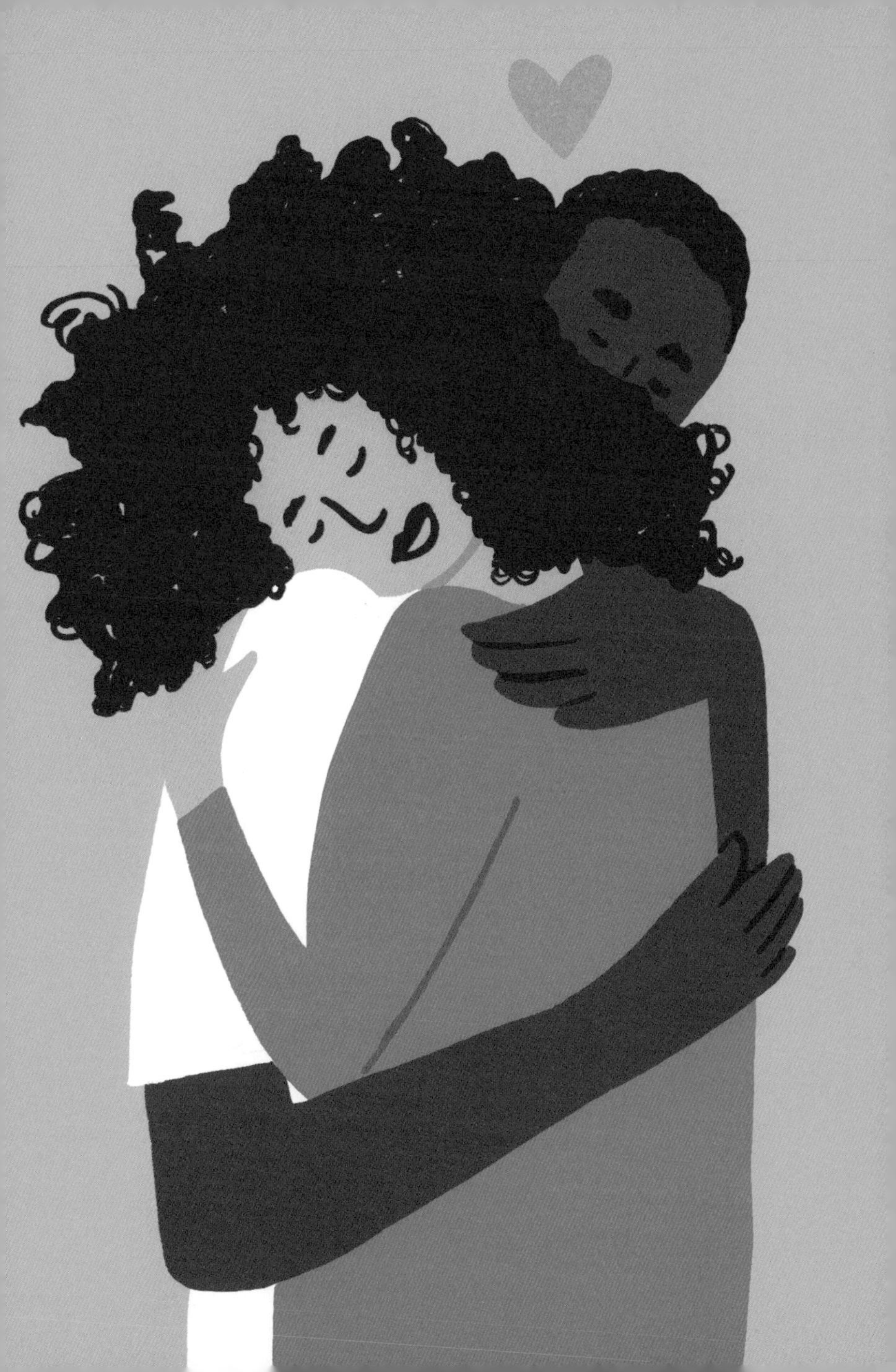

Our children
will be **BEAUTIFUL**:

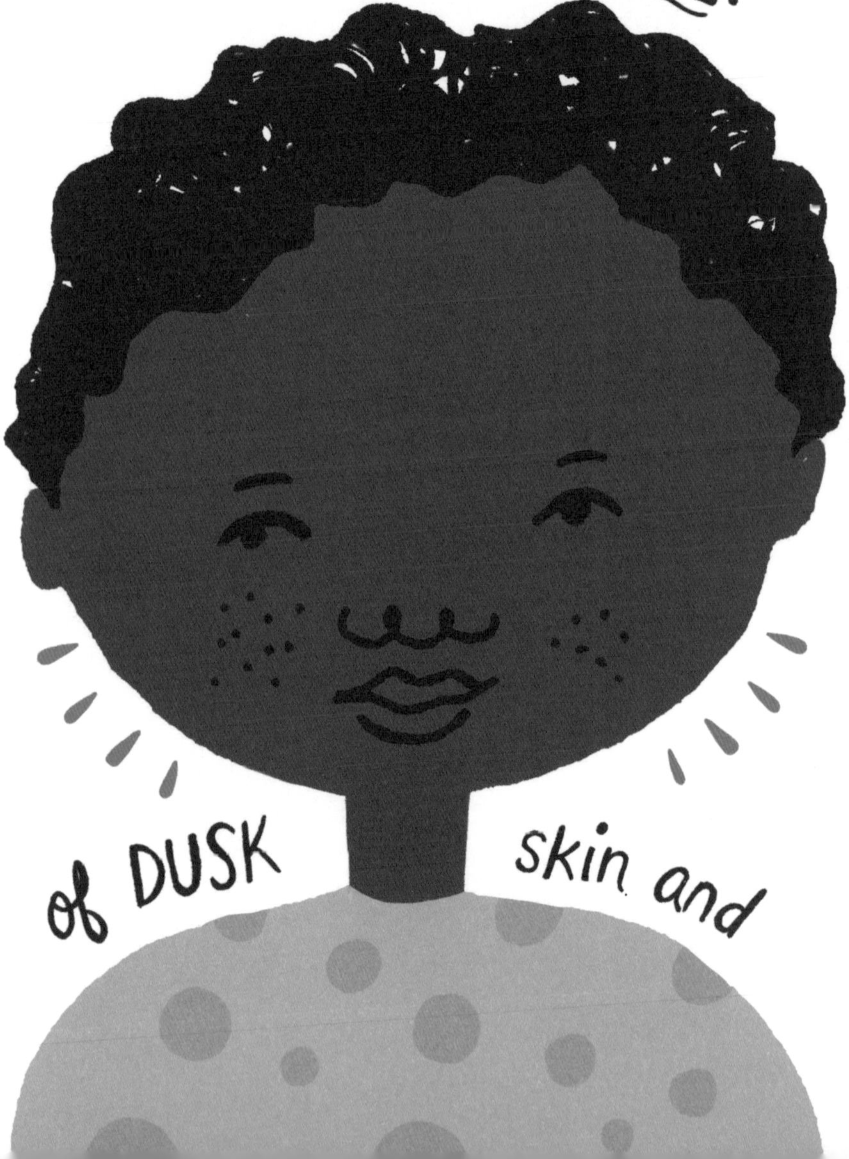

of DUSK skin and

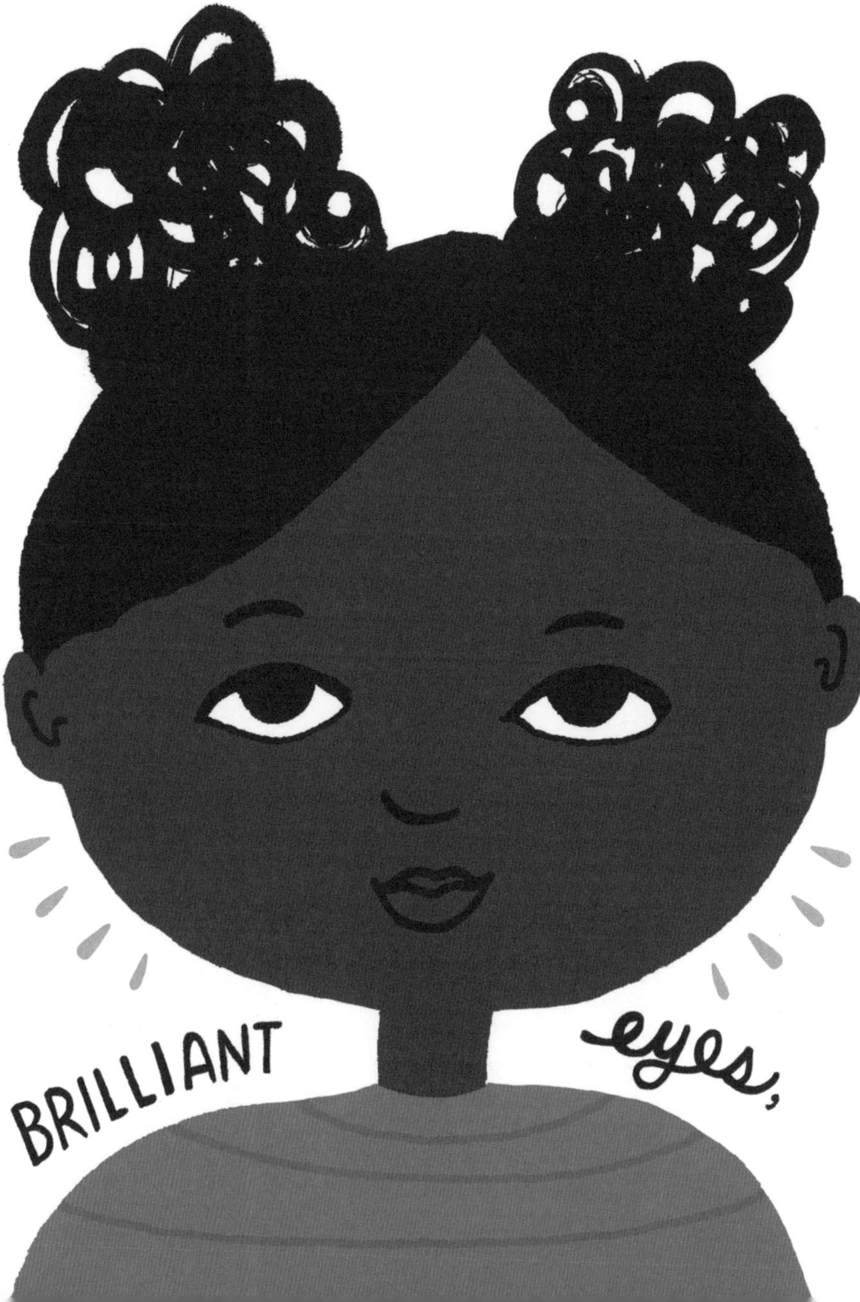

BRILLIANT eyes,

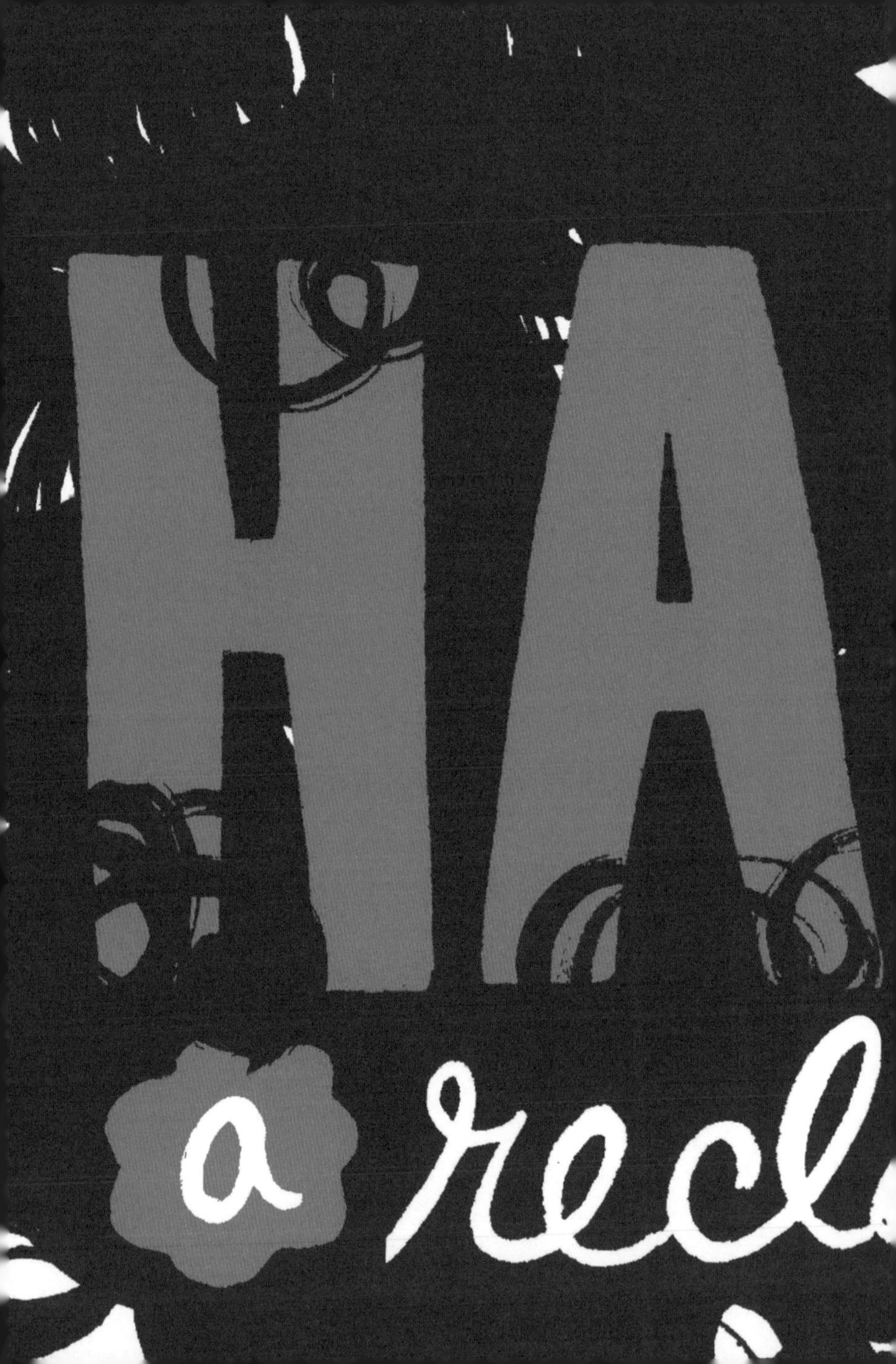
HA
a recl

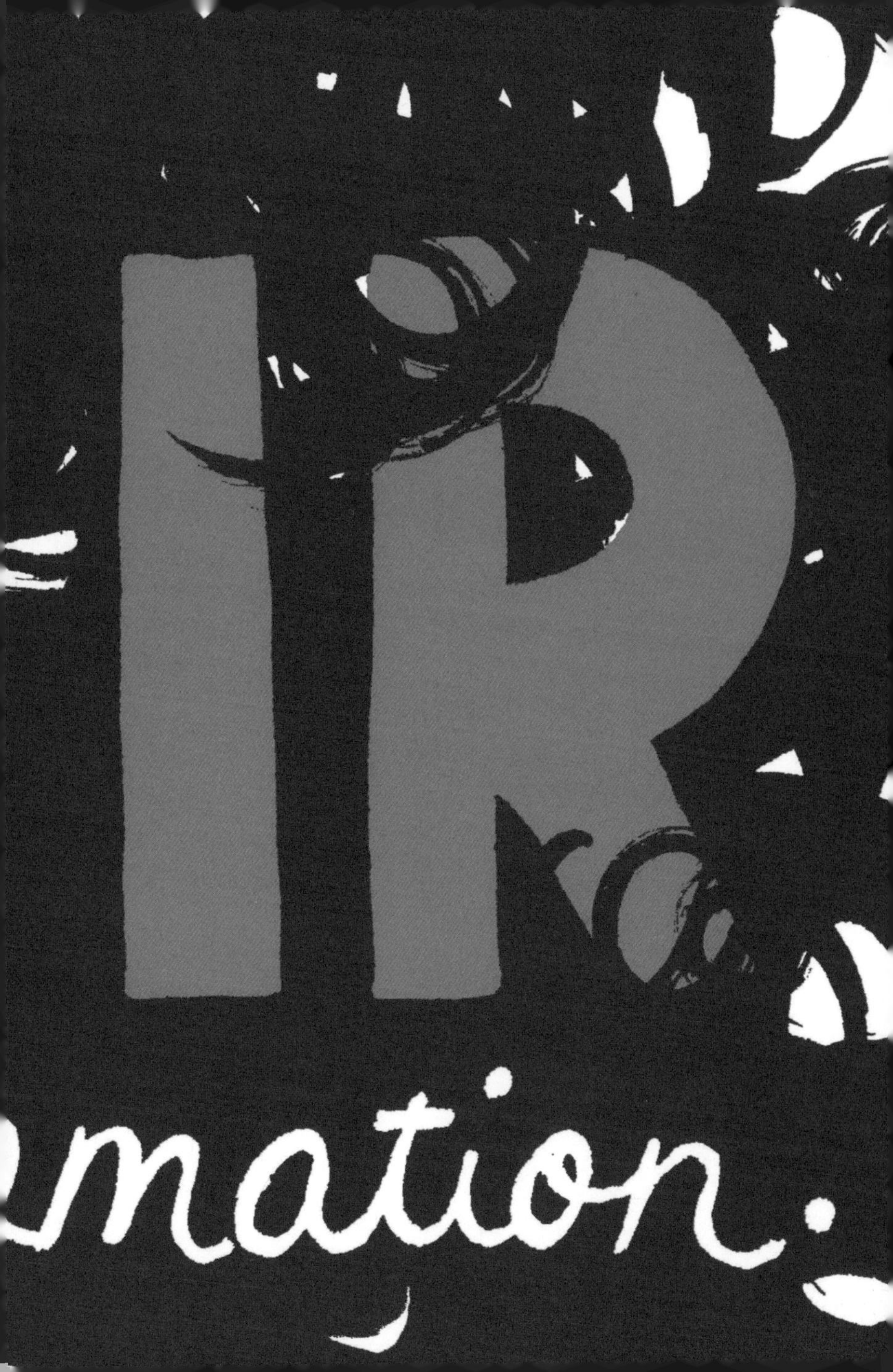
mation.

Oh, how I will braid

PRIDE

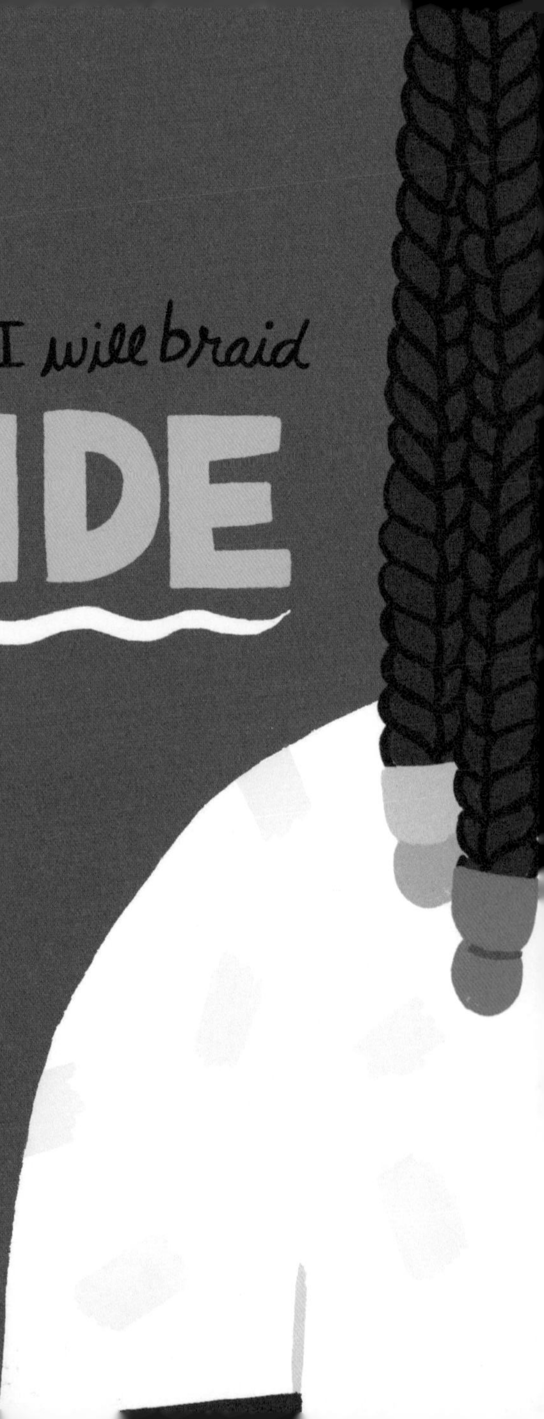

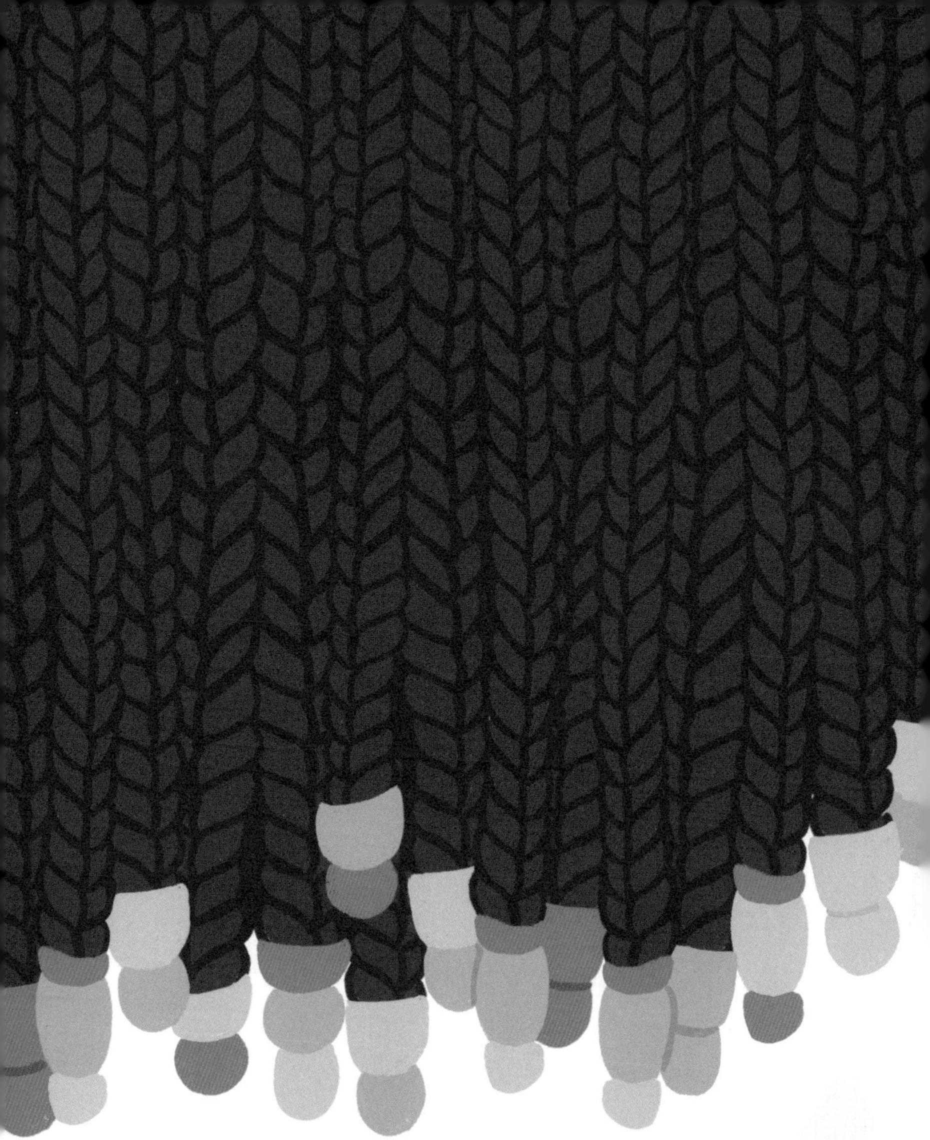

down their backs,
and from the moment
they leave the womb,

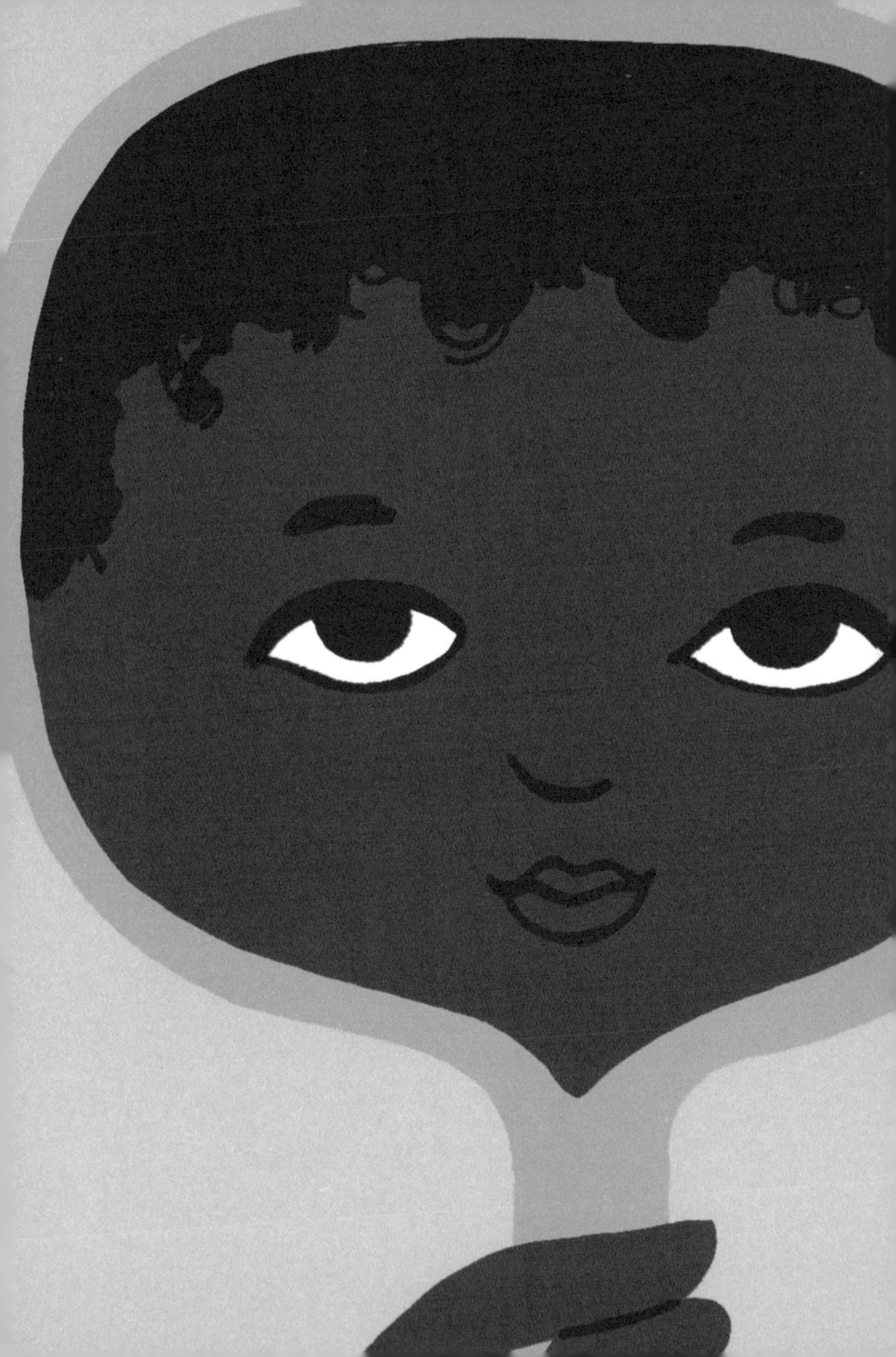

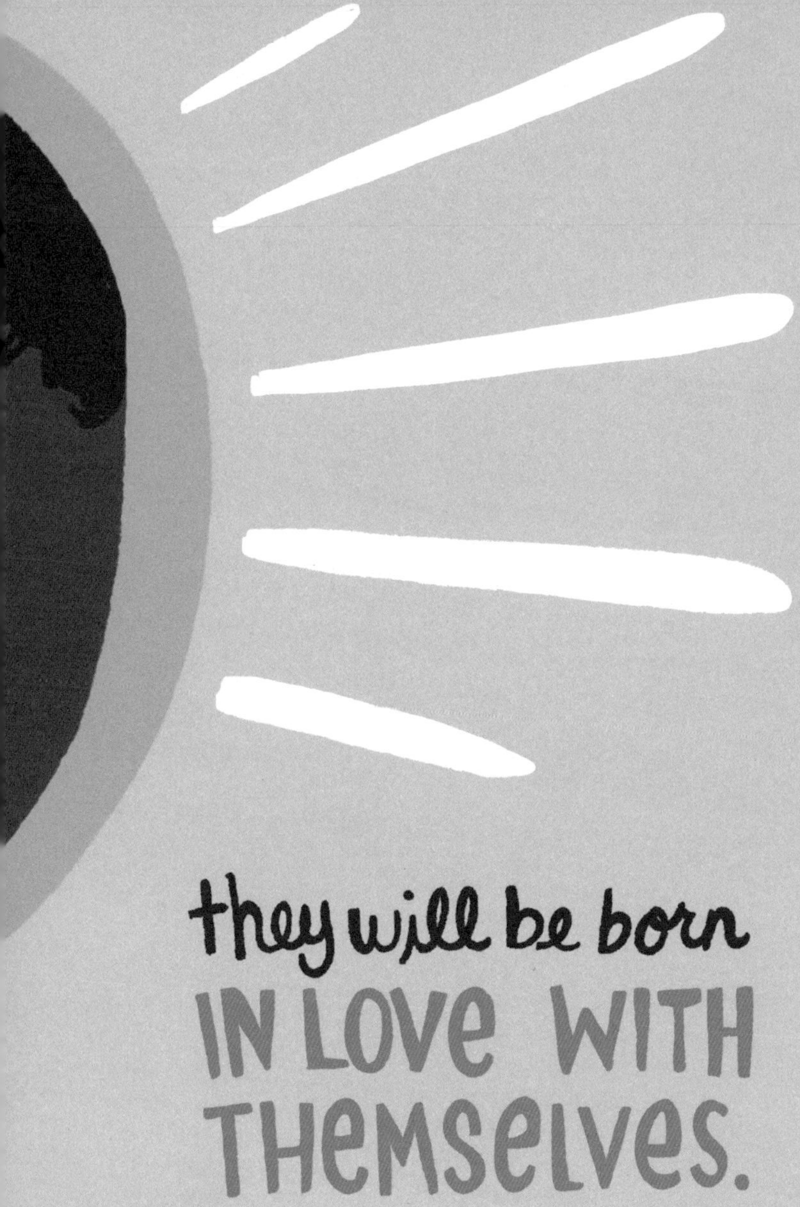

they will be born
IN LOVE WITH
THEMSELVES.

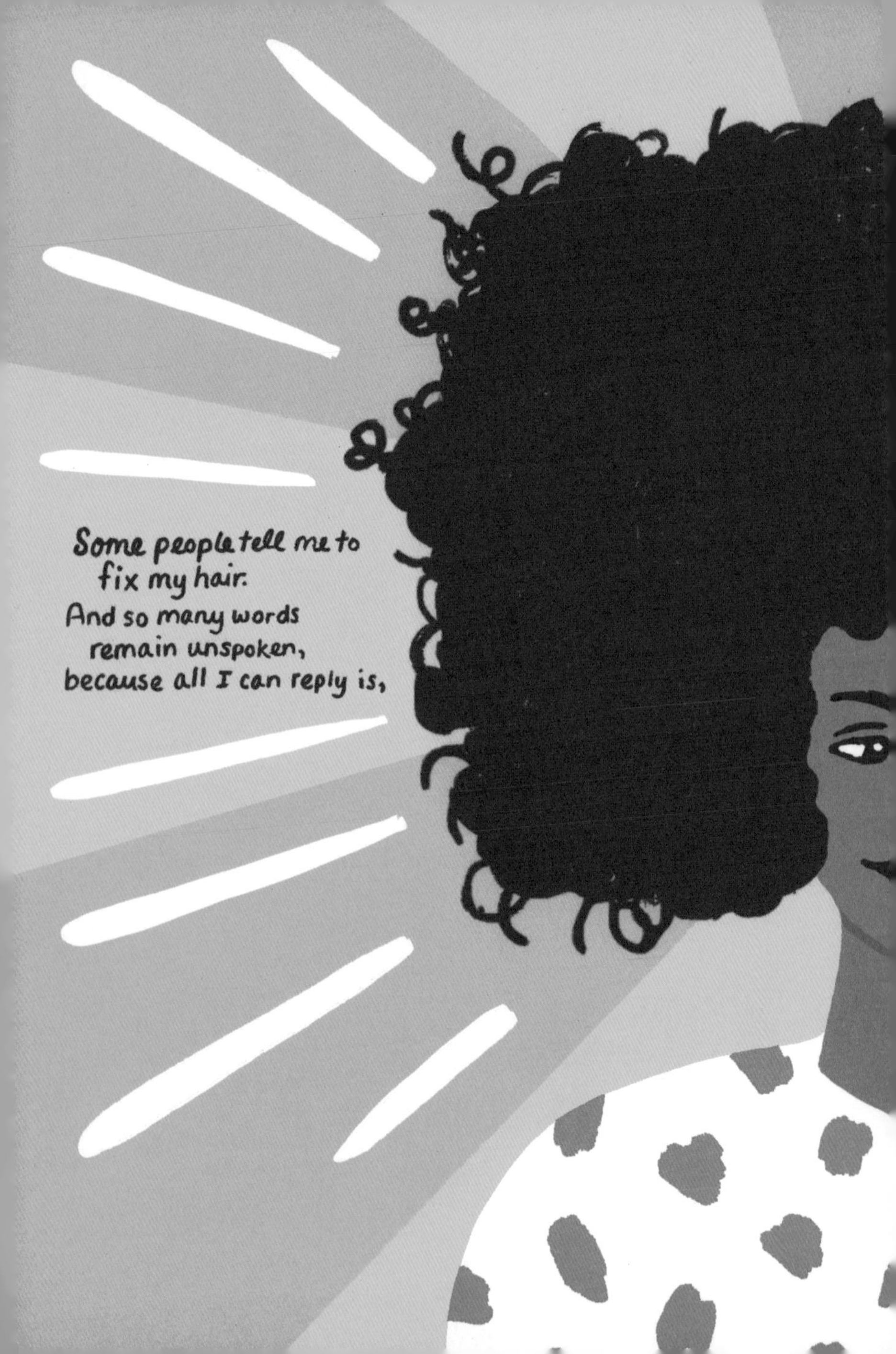

Some people tell me to
fix my hair.
And so many words
remain unspoken,
because all I can reply is,

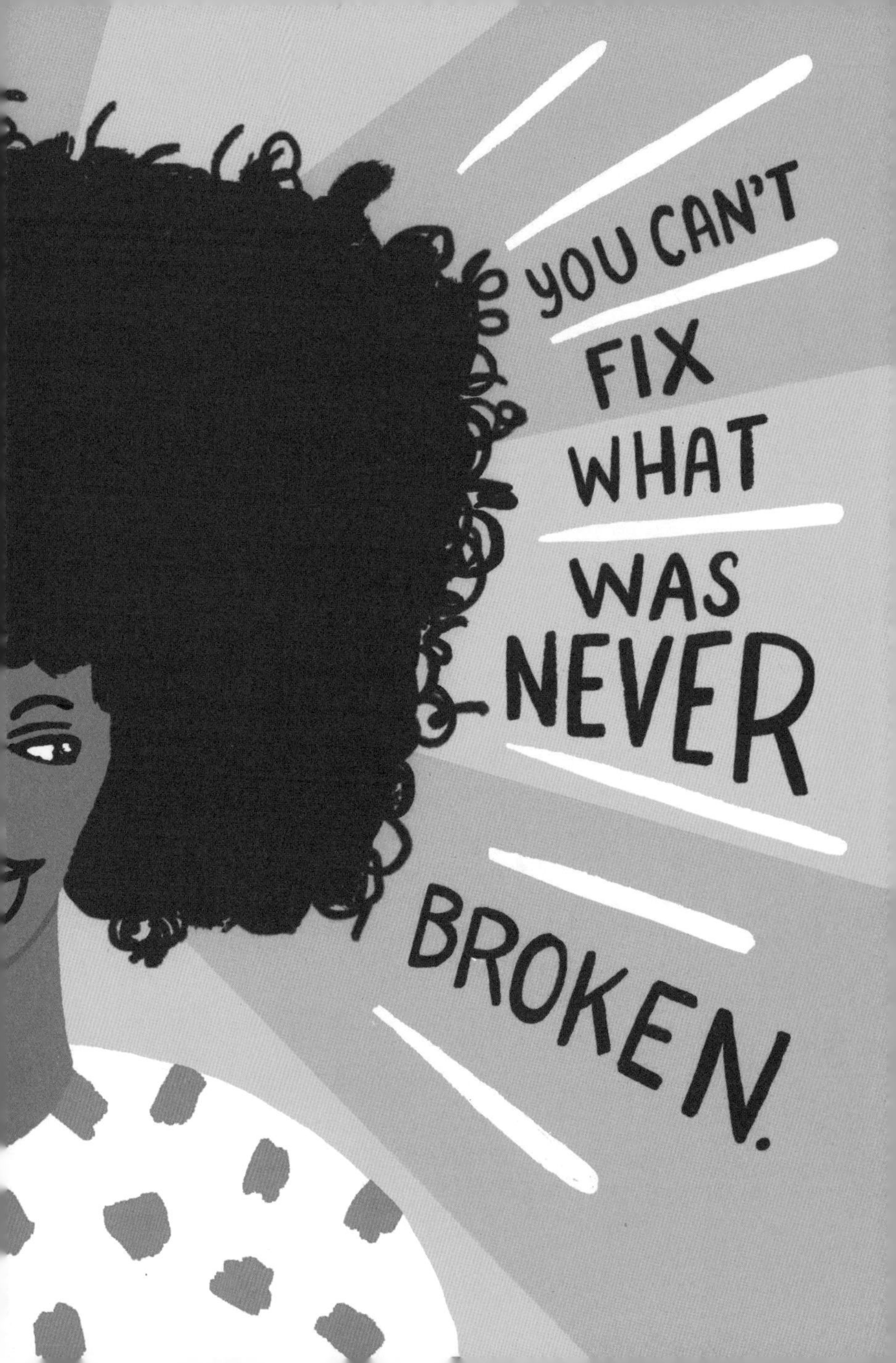
YOU CAN'T
FIX
WHAT
WAS
NEVER
BROKEN.

For Shakir Cannon-Moye and the futures for which we dream. —E.A.

To Maya Paloma: be free. —A.P.

Quill Tree Books is an imprint of HarperCollins Publishers.

Inheritance

For information address HarperCollins Children's Books, a division of HarperCollins Publishers, 195 Broadway, New York, NY 10007.
www.epicreads.com

ISBN 978-0-06-293194-8

The artist used a combination of hand-drawn elements and digital illustrations for this book.
Typography by Andrea Pippins
Art Direction by Erin Fitzsimmons
22 23 24 25 26 RTLO 10 9 8 7 6 5 4 3 2 1
First Edition